PENGUIN ANANDA

JYOTIRLINGAM

Amit Kapoor, PhD, is honorary chairman at Institute for Competitiveness, India, and lecturer at Stanford University, US. Amit is the author of bestsellers *The Elephant Moves: India's New Place in the World* (co-authored with Amitabh Kant), *Riding the Tiger: How to Execute Business Strategy in India* (co-authored with Wilfried Aulbur) and *The Age of Awakening: The Story of the Indian Economy since Independence*, all published by Penguin Random House India.

Bibek Debroy is a renowned economist, scholar and translator. He has worked in universities, research institutes, industry and for the government. He has widely published books, papers and articles on economics. As a translator, he is best known for his magnificent rendition of the Mahabharata in ten volumes as well as the three-volume Valmiki Ramayana—both of which have been published to wide acclaim by Penguin Classics. He is also the author of *Sarama and Her Children*, which splices his interest in Hinduism with his love for dogs.

JYOTIRLINGAM

SHIVA AND THE TWELVE COLUMNS OF LIGHT

AMIT KAPOOR | **BIBEK** DEBROY

PENGUIN
ANANDA

An imprint of Penguin Random House

PENGUIN ANANDA

Penguin Ananda is an imprint of the Penguin Random House group of companies whose addresses can be found at global.penguinrandomhouse.com

Published by Penguin Random House India Pvt. Ltd
4th Floor, Capital Tower 1, MG Road,
Gurugram 122 002, Haryana, India

First published in Penguin Ananda by Penguin Random House India 2024

Copyright © Amit Kapoor and Bibek Debroy 2024

Photos by Vibhav Kapoor and Conor Martin

10 9 8 7 6 5 4 3 2 1

The views and opinions expressed in this book are the authors' own and the facts are as reported by them which have been verified to the extent possible, and the publishers are not in any way liable for the same.

Please note that no part of this book may be used or reproduced in any manner for the purpose of training artificial intelligence technologies or systems.

ISBN 9780143470106

Typeset in Adobe Caslon Pro by Manipal Technologies Limited, Manipal
Printed at Thomson Press India Ltd, New Delhi

www.penguin.co.in

CONTENTS

INTRODUCTION

The realm of spirituality is a tapestry of beliefs and experiences. If one goes on to explore the meaning of spirituality, one will not come across a definite answer. That is precisely the essence of this realm. One cannot pinpoint the specific nature of spirituality, despite its association with a sense of connection to something greater than oneself, a search for meaning in life, and a quest for inner peace and transcendence. It varies widely, altering from culture to culture, and presenting itself to individuals in different ways. This book explores the intricacies of the spiritual path and the diverse ways in which individuals perceive and connect with the divine. Central to this exploration is Lord Shiva, a deity who is beyond the pale of any categorization. The essence of this book lies in its exploration of Shiva or the varied aspects of Shiva, through the lenses of different perspectives.

Contrary to the common practice of devoting each chapter to a particular theme or sub-theme, the following chapters defy traditional categorization. As we navigate this book, we traverse the landscape of the twelve sacred jyotirlingams viewed through distinct eyes.

The appeal of India's the twelve jyotirlingams extends far beyond national borders, drawing tourists from around the globe. Experiencing the jyotirlingams in person is a transcendental experience for many. Countless online reviews and travel accounts detail pilgrimages to these revered sites. Yet, amid the abundance of information available, there remains a notable scarcity of narratives capturing the deeply personal and unique experiences of these jyotirlingams, as eloquently documented in the pages of this book. The book captures a westerner's perspective as he embarks on a journey to witness the jyotirlingams first-hand. We get an insight into the experience of an individual detached from the cultural milieu of Hinduism through an immensely spiritual and personal journey. Offering a fresh perspective on the spiritual significance of these sacred sites, it presents readers with profound questions about spirituality, drawing from personal experiences at the jyotirlingams. The spiritual journey in India is bound to be different from the way it unfolds in the West. While the fundamental nature of spiritual journeys is universal, the specific physical and cultural context significantly influences the way these experiences unfold. When someone from the Western cultural context recounts a spiritual journey in a setting vastly different from their own, the observations and insights gained become particularly

Introduction

revealing. The unfamiliarity of the cultural landscape adds a layer of complexity to the spiritual narrative, offering unique perspectives and insights that may not have emerged in a more familiar environment. The book brings insights into how physical and cultural surroundings play a crucial role in shaping and enriching the spiritual quest.

Yet another meaningful perspective gets added through the lens of an artist, or more specifically, a photographer, both literally and metaphorically. Traversing the length and breadth of the twelve jyotirlingams, we get a glimpse of the visual narrative of Shiva's abodes. This chapter's uniqueness lies in the duality of perspective. On one hand, there's a sense of individuality that stems from the vantage point of a photographer who maintains a sense of detachment like an observer. On the other hand, there's also a shared or collective aspect to the experience. The goal of *darshana* (viewing a divine image/idol) is a collective communal pursuit. This dual role—that of an observer and a part of a larger collective with the common purpose of seeking darshana— is what brings to the reader a different outlook. Through this chapter, we witness the writer expressing how their journey across various locations in India, each with diverse symbolic representations of Shiva, has profoundly influenced their artistic and social philosophy. To further enrich these personal accounts and experiences of Shiva, the book offers insights into the stories of the jyotirlingams. It gives us a perspective on the intellectual facets of spirituality, providing a nuanced understanding of the sacred sites rooted in ancient texts. Each jyotirlingam is associated with a story, and this chapter shares these stories with the reader. It further conveys a rather powerful idea—the omnipresence of Shiva signifies that just as Shiva is omnipresent, his sacred lingams are also found everywhere. The book progresses to offer yet another unique exploration of the idea of Shiva. In a departure from the traditional perception of Shiva that often implies deity worship or includes typical narratives of perceiving the divine, the book challenges preconceptions and calls readers to think about the divide from an unusual vantage point. When a reader first opens a book on a topic they wish to explore, they may have preconceived expectations from the pages about to unfold. Each reader carries a set of expectations and assumptions about what the book might offer. The book may or may not align with what the reader may have predicted, and often, it is the latter that is more enriching. It is the deviations from initial expectations that make for a more insightful reading experience. It is where the content challenges, surprises and surpasses the reader's notions that highlights the transformative power of content. In this sense, this book offers an opportunity for the reader to embark on a profound journey of exploration. This book brings fresh perspectives to the jyotirlingams, and each perspective adds a distinct colour. These diverse narratives—Western, artistic, mythological, scholarly and atheistic—come together to paint a fuller or more holistic portrait of Shiva and the jyotirlingams. This speaks to the subjective nature of spiritual experiences, which are shaped by one's unique background and circumstances. While the subjective nature of spiritual experiences comes across in the journeys through the jyotirlingams and the exploration of the idea of Shiva, the book is grounded in the stories from the Puranas.

From the diverse thoughts, stories and experiences presented in this text, what stands out is the absence of a singular and definitive path to understanding the divine. A spiritual quest, as the word 'quest' implies, is a deeply personal pursuit. The jyotirlingams are beyond just sacred geographical sites; they are woven together through stories and their experience varies from individual to individual. Shiva is not limited to a singular narrative. In fact, through the following pages, Shiva emerges as a kaleidoscope of perspectives. In a world fraught with clashes resulting from rigid convictions, a literary piece exploring various facets of the divine, tied together by the spiritual experiences of individuals embedded in diverse social settings, becomes significant. The book demonstrates through its diverse chapters that the same God can be seen, felt and understood in vastly different ways. Be it through the viewpoint of a Westerner, an artist, a researcher of Hindu scriptures, an atheist or a scholar, each view contributes a unique colour to the canvas of spirituality. Throughout history, Shiva has been worshipped in varied forms. The worship of Shiva has taken on multifaceted expressions, but this book is not centred on Shiva worship. It is about the Shiva lingams, with a particular emphasis on the twelve jyotirlingams. Each jyotirlingam is revered as a radiant pillar of light, symbolizing Shiva's cosmic presence and transcendent power. Traditionally, the perception of religious visits has been rather limited. A shift from a merely ritualistic pursuit of *darshana* to a more profound and meaningful engagement with the journey helps develop a deeper understanding of the divine and, thus, oneself. The divine is best experienced through a blend of spiritual depth, narrative comprehension and a comprehensive understanding that transcends mere physical rituals. The book, therefore, invites the reader on an exploratory and reflective journey through a solid grounding in the stories around jyotirlingams and spiritual experiences.

THE IDEA OF SHIVA

AMIT KAPOOR

Encapsulating the boundless form of Shiva in words is indeed a mammoth task. This essay does not limit itself to elaborating on Shaivism or Lord Shiva in Hinduism in general. The term 'idea' in the title itself is an indicator of the fluidity of interpretation and formlessness associated with Shiva, which is the backbone of this piece. Before delving into the understanding of 'Shiva', touching upon how he is commonly represented and interpreted is a good starting point.

If you put forth to the world the question 'Who is Shiva?', these are some of the more common aspects that will form the answer.

One of the central deities in Hinduism, Shiva embodies a multifaceted and enigmatic concept within the religion. He is often referred to as the 'Destroyer' in the Hindu Trinity, alongside Brahma, the Creator and Vishnu, the Preserver, but the idea of Shiva, as elaborated in this essay, is far beyond this image of him as a 'Destroyer God'. He is both a fierce ascetic and a benevolent deity, symbolizing the dual nature of life. With his ash-covered body, flowing locks and third eye, he is also associated with various aspects of Hindu spirituality, such as meditation, yoga and the pursuit of inner peace. In Hinduism, Lord Shiva is depicted as an omniscient yogi who leads a modest life on Mount Kailash. With a third eye on his forehead, Lord Shiva is revered as one of the most formidable powers in the cosmos. His common depiction includes a serpent Vasuki coiled around his neck, a crescent moon adorning his head and the holy River Ganga flowing from his hair; the *trishula* (Shiva's trident) and *damaru* (drum) are his divine instruments and his throat is depicted as blue.[1] His multifaceted nature is reflected in the several manifestations he takes on, each representing a unique aspect of his nature that holds its own symbolic significance. Some of the prominent forms of Shiva include Rudra, Nataraja, Ardhanareeshvara, Bhairava, Pashupati, Mahakala, Rishabha, Gangadhara and Chandrashekara. Shiva lingam worship is a central practice in Shaivism. Revered as a symbol of the formless, infinite and all-pervading nature of Lord Shiva, devotees believe that it embodies divine energy and consciousness.

---

[1] *Trishula* is a trident and *damaru* is a drum, in the shape of an hourglass.

Kashi

However, what Shiva stands for goes far beyond a simple understanding of him as one of Hinduism's principal deities.

क्रिालाद्यनवच्छिन्नानन्त
चिन्मात्रमूर्तये ।
स्वानुभूत्येकमानाय
नम:शान्ताय तेजसे ॥
कालोऽयं निरवधि: ॥

Salute to the ever tranquil and effulgent one whose frame comprises solely by consciousness without frontiers that cannot be pierced by either space or time and whose presence can be felt only within the realm of our consciousness.

This is the basis of the essay's title—the 'idea' or 'understanding' goes beyond the auspices of any religion.

Literature abounds with various interpretations and practices associated with Shiva that followers hold. While Hinduism as a religion offers a multiplicity of forms of various deities and significant room for interpretation, the diversity of meanings attached to Shiva is peculiar. One way of perceiving this range of Shiva's multiple interpretations also reflects his greater relevance. Before delving into my view of Shiva, it is important to understand my viewpoint. A 'viewpoint' is situated in the context of one's life experiences. A 'view' is then better understood after gaining insights into the vantage point through which it is seen.

Traversing the Whole Spectrum

The philosophy of understanding the world around us goes back centuries. Throughout history, various philosophers and thinkers have contributed to this field of inquiry, adding to its breadth and complexity. This field encompasses various schools of thought and approaches. For instance, empiricism emphasizes the role of observation in gaining knowledge of the world around us; rationalism highlights the role of reasoning in acquiring knowledge; and naturalism emphasizes the importance of natural law and scientific investigation to explain the world around us and the rejection of any supernatural beliefs. These are some of the many fields that exist, each standing as a massive area of study. Each philosophical perspective provides a lens through which individuals and scholars can explore and make sense of the world around them. Some of these fields offer a limited perspective on making sense of the world. Empiricism, for example, tends to be limiting in more ways than one. It gives importance to observable phenomena, consequently relying on sensory perception and observation. Because of this, it becomes a flexible yardstick. What I may disprove today can be proven true tomorrow, when I have the means to measure it. This essentially means that empirical knowledge can evolve and change over time as new evidence becomes available.

Hence, there is a need to explore a belief system or a way of understanding the broader world.

When thought about in this manner, an atheist and a staunch religious believer are just two individuals with different ways of understanding the world around them. While this may seem like a simplistic abstraction, it lies at the very heart of the distinction between most schools of thought.

There exist numerous definitions of atheism. To put it simply, 'atheism' is a lack of belief in the existence of gods or deities. It is not a belief system or a religion itself, but rather a stance characterized by the absence of belief in the supernatural. What often characterizes the atheistic perspective is scepticism, rationality and an emphasis on evidence. Among the many definitions that exist, philosopher J.L. Schellenberg's approach to atheism sums it up concisely. He says that 'in philosophy, the atheist is not just someone who doesn't accept theism, but more strongly someone who opposes it'. Additionally, philosopher William L. Rowe states, 'Atheism is the position that affirms the nonexistence of God. It proposes positive disbelief rather than mere suspension of belief.' I have come to firmly challenge the existence of God, and I have supported this positive disbelief. Theism is a belief system that affirms the presence of one or more gods. It can take various forms, including monotheism (belief in one God), polytheism (belief in multiple gods) and henotheism (belief in one primary deity while acknowledging the existence of other gods). These are commonplace definitions of atheism and theism. Before I delve into the reasons why I call myself an atheist, I must define what I believe is 'theism'. I distinguish theism from atheism since the former stems from a 'belief system' and the latter is, beyond its affirmation in the non-existence of God, a quest for understanding. This quest inspired my idea of Shiva, as explored in detail in the subsequent section. It is an exploration of an idea or understanding. I see theism to be more aligned with a 'belief' and my atheism with 'seeking'.

Atheism, as my personal choice, stems from a few key reasons. One of these is a strong belief in rationality and an evidence-based understanding of the world. Being an economist whose life's work has been driven through evidence-based research backed by facts grounded in numbers, claims made by religious doctrines have failed to convince me of their truth. One of the key quests of human life lies in our journey to understand the world around us. I believe that scientific methods are reliable tools to do so. The other major reason is disillusionment and discontent with the way organized religion manifests in the world.

Throughout history, religion has played a pivotal role in influencing societies and individuals. It has had both positive and negative consequences. Religion offers people a sense of purpose and helps add meaning to people's lives. More importantly, it offers individuals a moral compass that can guide them to make ethical choices. Religion has also been vital in fostering a sense of community, belonging and compassion. Many religious organizations are deeply involved in charitable activities. Even places of worship can serve as centres for social cohesion, where people find emotional and social support during difficult times. However, religion is not without its negative aspects. One of the most significant drawbacks is the potential for division and conflict it can create. The impact of religion on individuals and societies is a complex interplay of both positive and negative aspects that vary greatly depending on specific beliefs and interpretations. I believe that it is important to highlight this dual nature of religion, where it can inspire acts of compassion, community and morality but also be associated with conflict and discrimination.

If we look at how organized religion has panned out in the world, there are various instances that show that it can be vulnerable to corruption and insincerity. The world has increasingly witnessed organized religion being susceptible to instances involving financial misconduct, superstitious practices and blind rather than genuine faith. For me, these issues have cast doubt on the authenticity of organized religion. Rather than promoting ideas of humility, selflessness and compassion, organized religion can become a channel to promote the contrary.

The connection between religion and violence is a contested area of discussion, with social scientists divided over the nature of this association. It is important to note that violence is a complex and multifaceted phenomenon. While there are numerous studies on religious violence, humanity has seen violence stemming from a variety of sources. For instance, in the name of civilization, countries have perpetrated violence against indigenous people. History has witnessed actions that have, prima facie, been motivated by a desire to promote democratic values but have also been criticized for contributing to violence and instability in certain regions. Thus, violence as a phenomenon can be attributed to a combination of individual, social, cultural, economic and political factors, and there can be multiple origins of violence.

Some scholars, like William Cavanaugh, argue that when religious texts and beliefs are employed to legitimize or rationalize one's actions, this violence is fundamentally not religious because it is a mere distortion of the religious teachings. However, another line of argument states that because religions foster certainties, they can often be a fundamental source of conflict. History is replete with examples of communities going to war over religion and of groups being persecuted in the name of religion. A telling statistic from Pew Research Center says that over a quarter of the nations across the globe encountered significant occurrences of conflicts driven by religious animosity, incidents of mob violence linked to religious factors, acts of terrorism rooted in religion and instances of women facing harassment due to violations of religious norms. Yet another major reason underlying my disengagement with religious beliefs is patriarchy in religion, which reflects the pervasive dominance of male authority and power within religious institutions, doctrines and practices across many world religions, including Christianity, Islam, Judaism, Hinduism and Buddhism. Men have traditionally held leadership roles, interpreted sacred texts and shaped religious teachings, playing the role of custodians of religion. Throughout history, this has excluded and subordinated women in religious hierarchies. There have been many instances where religious

Srisailam

texts have been interpreted in a way that not only justifies gender-based discrimination but also promotes it. Thus, organized religion and its ills are one of the key reasons why I was driven to explore atheistic beliefs. My belief in Shiva is a spiritual and philosophical pursuit, separate from any organized religion.

From a believer at twenty-five to an atheist at forty, the arc of my journey has been marked by certain perplexing experiences that are impossible to categorize or label. The reason why I call my experience a journey from one end of the spectrum to another is because I am not merely an atheist but a staunch believer-turned-atheist. At twenty-five, my belief in religion and the very existence of God was unshakeable. This faith was not something that stemmed from my outside world. It came from my unique individual spiritual experiences, which can be considered the rarest of the rare. One could call them spiritual experiences, but I believe they are beyond definition and reason. 'Reason' has its own limitations. In this context, Immanuel Kant's line of thought on reasoning comes to mind. He pointed to certain strict limits that reasoning has. In *The Critique of Pure Reason* (1781), Kant highlights that reason alone cannot provide us with insights into God or a realm that exists beyond our sensory perceptions. In my early twenties, it was the realm beyond reason that presented itself to me in its full glory.

These experiences are hard to pen—whether it was me holding immense knowledge of a subject without knowing the source of it or its acquisition, the ability to see that which was beyond sight or feel elements that were beyond any stretch of imagination. When I went to Lucknow for my PhD, I happened to come across an entity telling me its intent was to end my life. I responded with an unwavering firmness, stating that it wasn't time yet and that I would know when it would be the right time, as Shiva told me that I was here for a certain period. Yet another experience of mine that is mystifying and significant in my life is learning astrology at the age of seventeen. At that tender age, I was fascinated by the field's study of cosmic influences on human life and wanted to learn from an Aghori. The learning did not happen over a period. In fact, he, as a teacher, passed the knowledge of the field in its entirety to me with just a pat on the back. This process is a mystery to me as well. But after that instance, it was as though the knowledge of astrology was inherent. This knowledge enabled me to see people and the paths that lay ahead of them. This also meant that I could see death. My first incident of seeing death ahead of its time was in the case of my grandfather. I expressed to my father my understanding that my grandfather would not be there anymore the next day. He felt I was overthinking. However, it so happened that my grandfather did pass away the very next day. This was when I began to deeply feel the downside of what I could see. Unfortunately, this wasn't the last of the ends I could sense for my near and dear ones. When my brother was hospitalized and the doctors had expressed confidence in his recuperation, I could sense, deep down, that it wasn't going to unfold that way. I told my wife that he was going to pass away, and he did. While witnessing the death of one's loved ones is painful, seeing it coming is even more painful.

Some experiences showed me the power of healing. My sister had a difficult pregnancy. She was hospitalized and in a serious condition. I was physically away from her, but even on a phone call with my mother, who was around her, I could tell certain things that would be impossible to know without being present in that hospital. When I visited my sister in person, all I remember was touching her hands. She was soon on the path of recovery. There have also been times when I have seen Shiva in my dreams and have woken up, feeling a cathartic sense of bliss, an emotion I also felt after I visited the temple of Tirupati. Some may call it strong intuition or may even dismiss it. The truth of the matter was that these inexplicable experiences perplexed me because they were events I did not will into existence. As a child, despite being encouraged by my family to chant mantras out loud, I would never do so. At religious gatherings, where everyone would chant together, I'd never join them in chanting out loud. It is said that chanting a mantra in one's mind, rather than vocalizing it, amplifies its power. While I was not privy to this idea as a child, I have always chosen to go over *mantra*s in my mind.

It is against this backdrop of my personal journey, including my belief in atheism, driven mainly by disillusionment and discontent with organized religion, rationality and my personal experiences, that my idea of Shiva comes forth. I see the genesis of this book emerging from the day my son, Vibhav, was born. It was 14 February

1999. We were expecting his birth a week later, as confirmed by the doctors. However, I was confident that he would be born the very next day, on Maha Shiva Ratri, and he did come into the world that day. I see him as an *ansha* (portion) of Shiva who manifested through me. This book is my journey to the jyotirlingams through the eyes of my son, Vibhav.

My experiences instilled in me an insatiable hunger for exploring the idea of Shiva. This context of my life has shaped my view of Shiva, and, in turn, Shiva has shaped my life.

Shiva in the Fullest of Glory

Time is one of the cornerstones of my understanding of Shiva's form. Shiva is often referred to as Mahakaala. Shiva and time can also be considered synonymous, with him being referred to as *aadi* (beginning) and *anta* (end). The underlying notion is that Shiva, in his boundless nature, is time, stretching eternally into the past and the future. The association of Shiva with Mahakaala highlights several aspects of his divine nature. It showcases the aspect of timelessness, of Shiva being beyond the limitations of time as we perceive it. He embodies the eternal and unchanging aspect of existence. Shiva, thus, can be associated with transcendence beyond the material world. These understandings question our idea of time. A recent study challenges the prevailing cosmological model and suggests that our universe might be twice as old as it is currently believed. The study proposes that the universe is approximately 26.7 billion years old, in contrast to the previous estimate of 13.7 billion years. This goes to show that to say our understanding of time is limited is an understatement. Everything is finite in the vastness of time, including the universe. To quote K. Sivaraman from *Saivism in Philosophical Perspective* (1973): 'The world exists in time and ceases to exist in time.' The universe may cease to be, but time remains, as does its greatness. Time knows no bounds and is without beginning or end. It is thus timeless. We can further put the vastness of time into perspective by further quoting from *Saivism in Philosophical Perspective*:

The belief underlying the conception of God as the universal Destroyer (*sarva-samhara-kartd*) rests on the insight that all things of the universe, the inert objects, classes or species of lives, the life of the individual, the history of the group and the nation, the course of the cosmos with its immense conglomerations of stars and nebulae and galaxies—all alike arc subject unexceptionally to the general process of termination and re-emanation. Everything of the natural and the cultural world, of the corporeal and the non-corporeal world, of the spoken and the speech-world is involved in inexorable change. Not only the visible spheres of the universe but all conceivable spheres of being even those of the highest world become resolved into their cause. Even gods as part of the corporeal world are subject to the general rule of absorption and re-emanation. A hundred million creator gods have perished and so have as many a million conserving gods/Time too paradoxically is involved in that process: it passes or lapses and re-emerges.

This is a rather humbling proposition. The idea that even gods perish in the vastness of time challenges all reality as perceived by beings. Time, then, could be considered the one true reality and the only permanence. Shiva, as Mahakaala, is this sole permanence.

Kashi

Shiva is also liberating; yet another aspect of his nature that is commonly highlighted is 'destruction'. Shiva is often regarded as the God of destruction, a crucial aspect of the divine Trinity, alongside Brahma, the Creator, and Vishnu, the Preserver. But in this context, the idea of Shiva gets narrow if he is perceived merely as the 'Destroyer God'. Here, we must view destruction in the context of two significant aspects: destruction as liberation and destruction as creation. Destruction, if seen from the perspective of death, is the only true eventuality. Birth implies death. From the moment one is born, death becomes impending. Everything else in a lifetime is unpredictable. One's death is the only event that is certain. Deeply ingrained and well understood, this thought makes one acutely aware of life's impermanence. There was an understanding in my family that, when a death occurs, we must not take our children to the cremation ground. However, I have not followed this with my children because I firmly believe that they should be aware of the impermanence of life as the ultimate reality and the only real certainty. This is the gateway to seeking liberation. One can also look at destruction, death or the end as liberation from a philosophical perspective. Existentialism and certain Eastern philosophies are among multiple schools of thought that touch upon the notion of death being liberating. The Advaita Vedanta, expounded by philosophers like Adi Shankaracharya, is noteworthy in this context. While putting it simply does not do justice to the colossal richness of this school of thought; for the sake of simplicity, it can be said that Advaita Vedanta proposes that ultimate liberation is achieved with the oneness of the individual soul with the *brahman*.[2] The physical body is viewed as transient and merely a vessel holding the eternal soul. Death is the shedding of the physical body. With the oneness of the soul and the brahman, one can attain liberation from the cycle of birth and death. Buddhism discusses nirvana in a similar context. It views life as characterized by suffering, with Nirvana being the ultimate goal—a state of liberation from suffering. It emphasizes the impermanent nature of things. Freedom can stem from understanding the finite nature of life. Thus, it is possible to find freedom in the idea of destruction. These are some lines of thought that equate death/destruction with liberation, offering us deeper insights into the idea of Shiva as liberation through destruction.

Creative Destruction

'Creation' forms the basis of this other line of thought that takes us beyond Shiva as the 'Destroyer God'. Destruction has been the foundation of creation. When the physical body dies, it decomposes and becomes one with nature to further become a part of life and its creations.

Even agriculture, one of humankind's most significant practices, required humans to first clear out forests. In fact, agriculture is the leading cause of deforestation, as human

---

[2] It is impossible to satisfactorily translate *brahman*, also known as *paramatman*, in English. This is the supreme *atman*, the supreme force, the supreme consciousness.

activities primarily involve clearing forests to create space for cultivating crops and establishing pastures for livestock. For life to grow from a seed, it must first disintegrate into soil. In fact, destruction preceded some of the world's major creations, including the formation of Earth itself. These examples serve as a testament to the significance of the end of the old for the emergence of the new. The idea of Shiva embodies this cyclical nature of the world. Death and destruction pave the way for re-creation and regeneration. Sivaraman calls destruction a 'necessary characteristic of productibility'.

In the context of Shiva as creation, the Shiva lingam is a sacred symbol that represents Shiva. It symbolizes the union of cosmic and feminine energies and the formless aspect of Shiva. Sadly, the phallic form of the Shiva lingam often attracts displeasure, or worse still, disgust. People express repulsion towards the Shiva lingam because of its form. It is important to dismiss such views by speaking about what they actually represent and urging people to explore this idea. The shape of the lingam, symbolizing the infinite, and the *yoni*, representing the cosmic womb, together form the source of all creation. They embody the union of Shiva's cosmic energy (lingam) and Shakti's feminine energy (yoni), representing the potential for creation and regeneration. It is the process of procreation that moves civilization forward. It is in this process of procreation that I see Shiva. Thus, when one creates another being, one embodies God. Nature has ordained us to play the role of creation, and species play God when they procreate. There

Trimbakeshwar

is another crucial aspect that the lingam bears. Just as its form does not have a beginning, a middle or an end, there is no finality to knowledge. Shiva stands for this constant pursuit of knowledge, creation, love and compassion. Shiva tells you to expand your horizons continuously, as an individual and as a civilization. The pursuit of science and philosophy is the same. In the context of pursuing knowledge, it is important to understand that philosophy, science and spirituality are not mutually exclusive. Both science and philosophy try to understand the idea of creation and existence—one does so through experimentation and the other through thinking.

When We Meet, *How* Do We Meet?

People often think about and discuss meeting God. They often think about the 'when' of it—the hour of this meeting—and the 'what' of it—what one would say to God. I wish to take this a step further and ponder the 'how' of it. How would one meet God? How would I meet Shiva? Will it be a meeting of reverence or one of love? Most importantly, will we be equals?

अहं ब्रह्मास्मि (*Aham Brahmasmi*) is a profound Sanskrit phrase that translates to 'I am brahman', thus encapsulating the idea that the individual self is ultimately identical to the universal consciousness or the oneness between the two. If there is truth in this, then the meeting with Shiva must be a meeting of equals where I sit across from him and talk to him, not in awe of him but as an equal. I believe that if he exists, he will meet me at my final destination. When death comes upon me, I would like to be with Shiva in Varanasi. I have an unshakeable faith in this.

Just like Shiva's transcendent form, which cannot be explained, captured, limited, bound or demarcated, our quest for truth can be a constant. What is the idea of Shiva, then? Could there be a finite definition for an infinite form? In a world that has forever been obsessed with watertight compartments and definitions, Shiva drives an important message home: There may not be a clear answer to everything. There may not be an end to the quest for knowledge. Maybe this quest itself is the end.

This age-old verse from the *Isha Upanishad* elucidates the essence of our cosmic order and the idea of Shiva.

ॐ पूर्णमदः पूर्णमिदं पूर्णात्पुर्णमुदच्यते
पूर्णस्य पूर्णमादाय पूर्णमेवावशिष्यते ॥
ॐ शान्तिः शान्तिः शान्तिः ॥

*That (there) is complete/infinite, This (here) is complete/
infinite. Completeness arises from completeness. If completeness
is taken away from completeness. Only completeness remains.
Om, peace, peace, peace*

The universe possesses inherent and boundless wholeness. Every element of creation, emerging from this entirety, is complete by itself. Completeness exists both in the creator and within us.

As shared with Shivani Kowadkar.

References

Doniger, W. (2014). *On Hinduism*. Oxford University Press.

P. Draper. 2022. 'Atheism and Agnosticism'. In Stanford Encyclopedia of Philosophy. Retrieved October 3, 2023, from https://plato.stanford.edu/entries/atheism-agnosticism/#DefiAthe

K. Sivaraman.1973. *Saivism in Philosophical Perspective*. Varanasi, India: Bhargava Bhushan Press, published by Sundarlal Jain for Motilal Banarsidass.

G. Williams. 2023. 'Kant's account of Reason'. In Stanford Encyclopedia of Philosophy. Available at: https://plato.stanford.edu/entries/kant-reason/#ReasEmpiTrut

Rowe, W. L. (2000). Atheism. In E. Craig (Ed.), Concise Routledge Encyclopaedia of Philosophy (pp. 62–63). London and New York: Routledge.

World Economic Forum. 2019. 'Religious violence is on the rise. What can faith-based communities do about it?'. Retrieved October 3, 2023, from https://www.weforum.org/agenda/2019/02/how-should-faith-communities-halt-the-rise-in-religious-violence/

THE BIG ESSAY ON
JYOTIRLINGAM

BIBEK DEBROY

Introduction

When it comes to grammar, most languages, including Sanskrit, have three genders—masculine, feminine and neuter. The word '*lingam*' (लिङ्गम्) belongs to the neuter gender.

What does the word mean? The structure of the Sanskrit language is completely different from that of English. In Sanskrit, the meaning of every noun or pronoun is derived from the verbal root. The word *bibek, viveka* in Sanskrit, has no meaning until one recognizes that the verbal root '*vic*' means to separate or discriminate. Thus, viveka comes to mean discrimination or discernment. Many people, even educated Indians, are more exposed to Priapus than to their Sanskrit roots. Therefore, we readily translate lingam as penis, phallic symbol or the male genital organ. Greek roots have had a greater influence on us than our own. Every classical Indian musician knows the meaning of *lina*. The word means to merge or dissolve, and *lina-gamaka* is the soft merging of one note into another. Etymologically, lingam has the verbal root lina. A lingam is something into which everything merges. Words are not always used in their correct etymological sense.

Words can have multiple meanings. In any Sanskrit dictionary, the first meaning of the word lingam will be a mark or sign, not a genital organ. Let's take a few examples.

In Sanskrit grammar, as I said earlier, there are three genders: *pullingam* (masculine), *strilingam* (feminine) and *napumsakalingam* (neuter). Many Indian languages follow similar grammar patterns, and most people study grammar in school. The relevant textbooks do not refer to the masculine gender as the masculine phallic symbol, the feminine gender as the feminine phallic symbol and the neuter gender as the neuter phallic symbol. We recognize that lingam means gender. There are texts in Sanskrit that are a combination of a dictionary and a thesaurus. One of the more famous ones, but not the only one, is known as *Amarakosha*. It was composed by Amarasimha, probably around 400 CE and is still studied. It is referred to as *Amarakosha* after the author's name. The actual name of the text is *Namalinganushasanam* (नामलिङ्गानुशासनम्), the manual (*anushasanam*) on nouns (name) and gender (lingam). No one has yet incorporated a phallic symbol when translating it.

Kashmir had a tradition known as Kashmir Shaivism or Trika Shaivism, which integrated the worship of Shiva and Shakti with tantra. Abhinavagupta (975–1025 CE) is probably the most famous exponent. In this tradition, there is a text known as *Malinivijayottaratantra* (Malini Vijaya Uttara Tantra), subsequently quoted by Abhinavagupta in his *Tantraloka*. Chapter 18 of this text is on the conduct of yogis, and the seventy-seventh shloka in this chapter refers to lingam in conjunction with the name and *gotra* (lineage) of the yogi, relative to those of other yogis.[1] In other words, just as name and gotra identified the yogi, so did lingam, which was the mark of the sect. Samkhya, associated with the name of the sage Kapila, is one of the six *darshanaas* (schools of philosophy), the other five being Nyaya, Vaisheshika, Yoga, Purva Mimamsa and Vedanta. Among the earliest Samkhya texts to survive is *Samkhyakarika*, authored by Ishvara Krishna in the fourth or fifth century CE. There too, we will find the word lingam used in the sense of mark. Anything manifest is a lingam, as in mark, of the unmanifest. Words to that effect.[2] *Mahabhashya* is attributed to Patanjali, circa 250 BCE. This is a commentary on Panini's grammar. Anyone who has studied Sanskrit, especially Sanskrit grammar, will recognize the expression किंचिल्लिङ्गमासज्य वक्ष्यामि. What does this mean? Loosely translated, it means: 'I will speak about some lingams that are attached.' The word lingam is again used in the sense of an indicative sign or mark.

---

[1] Since most people are not aware of this, it is best to quote this part of the shloka—परस्वरूपलिङ्गादि नामगोलादिकं च यत्।

[2] The tenth shloka of *Samkhyakarika* is an example.

Therefore, one shouldn't be violent towards etymology and grammar. Lingam means a mark or a sign. The fact that some people, incorrectly, take it to be a penis is neither here nor there. When worshipping Shiva's lingam and visiting it, it's important to focus on the image or the iconography in a picture. There is a base or pedestal, known as *pitham*. In a typical image, the lingam will extend below the pitham, a detail we often fail to notice. The bit that extends below the pedestal represents Vishnu and Brahma. Brahma will be right at the bottom and Vishnu will be above Brahma.[3] The Shiva bit, above the pedestal, will usually be circular. With sexual connotations in mind, not only is the lingam thought of as a penis, but the pitham is thought of as a vagina. If that's the case, it would be odd to have the Vishnu and Brahma sections below it. Surely, if the intention is penetration, the penis appears to be pointing in the wrong direction. Pitham can at best be translated as seat or pedestal, never as a vagina. To bring in a vagina, one would have to use the word yoni. But the word yoni doesn't only mean vagina. It also means origin, womb, receptacle and seat. Being fixated on the vagina alone displays a one-track mind. Besides, in actual images or iconography, the pitham can be in the shape of a circle, ellipse, oblong, triangle, square, hexagon, octagon, dodecagon and even a hexadecagon. Some of these are odd shapes for a vagina.

---

[3] The shape of the Brahma section may a quadrilateral, while that of the Vishnu section may be an octagon.

Shiva has been worshipped for thousands of years in many different forms. The most recognizable form is indisputably the Shiva lingam. Shiva lingams, and not merely other forms of Shiva, have been found in excavations of the Sindhu-Sarasvati civilization. However, this book is not about Shiva worship; it specifically focuses on Shiva's lingams and the twelve jyotirlingams. How should we understand the word lingam? The ninth shloka in Chapter 6 of the *Shvetashvatara Upanishad* is beautiful enough to be quoted in its entirety.

न तस्य कश्चित् पतिरस्ति लोके न चेशिता नैव च तस्य लिङ्गम् ।
स कारणं करणाधिपाधिपो न चास्य कश्चिज्जनिता न चाधिपः ॥

In this world, no one is his master. No one has any control over him. He has no lingam. He is the cause. He is the lord of the sense organs. No one has fathered him. No one is his lord.[4] This is an excellent description of Shiva in his *nirguna* form. Shiva is not manifest. He is *avyakta*. He is without attributes or *gunas* (nirguna).[5] Nirguna and Avyakta Shiva are impossible for most people to grasp and comprehend. Therefore, Shiva also manifests himself in different forms. This is the *vyakta* aspect. This is also *saguna*, with gunas or attributes. The lingam is an expression of Vyakta and Saguna Shiva.

---

[4] Translations are my own.

[5] The *gunas* are sattva (purity), *rajas* (passion) and *tamas* (darkness). *Saguna* is an entity with these attributes. *Nirguna* is an entity without these attributes, indeed one to whom these notions don't apply.

The word *suktam* literally means 'good saying'. The word *stotram* refers to a chant or hymn of praise. But the two words, suktam and stotram, are often used interchangeably. Thousands of years of Shiva worship naturally led to suktams or stotrams being addressed to Shiva, describing his attributes, deeds and names. One such is *Shatarudriya* (addressed to 100 Rudras), from the *Vajasaneyi Samhita* associated with the *Shukla Yajur Veda*. Yet another is the *Shri Rudram* from the *Taittiriya Samhita* associated with the *Krishna Yajur Veda*.[6] Do these three mantras sound familiar? We hear them chanted all the time, with ॐ pre-fixed. (1) शिवाय नमः। This is perhaps the most familiar and is known as the Panchakshara or Pancharna Mantra since there are five (pancha) syllables (*akshara* or *arna)* in it; (2) तत्पुरुषाय विद्महेमहादेवाय धीमहि । तन्नोरुद्रः प्रचोदयात् ॥ This is the Mahadeva (Shiva) variant of the Gayatri mantra; (3) त्र्यंबकं यजामहेसुगन्धिं पुष्टिवर्धनम् । उर्वारुकमिव बन्धनान्मृत्योर्मुक्षीय माऽमृतात् ॥ This is the Mahamriyunjaya Mantra. A mantra may occur in more than one text. However, the earliest occurrence of these three mantras is in the *Taittiriya Samhita*, though there are mantras from the *Vajasaneyi Samhita* and *Shvetashvatara Upanishad* too. It is difficult, if not impossible, to date these texts satisfactorily. Roughly, 500 BCE is a good guess.

For more on lingams, we need to go back around 1000 years to the time of the Itihasa Purana. The term *itihasa* refers to the Ramayana (meaning the Valmiki Ramayana) and Mahabharata, while there are eighteen Maha (major)

---

[6] Rudra is another name for Shiva, and *Yajur Veda* has two branches, Shukla and Krishna.

Puranas.[7] There are references to Shiva in both the Valmiki Ramayana and Mahabharata. However, for stories about lingams, we should turn to the Maha Puranas. The Valmiki Ramayana was composed by Valmiki. After composing the Mahabharata, Krishna Dvaipayana Vedavyasa composed eighteen Maha Puranas. These eighteen are *Agni, Bhagavata, Brahma, Brahmanda, Brahmavaivarta, Garuda, Kurma, Linga, Markandeya, Matsya, Narada, Padma, Shiva, Skanda, Vamana, Varaha, Vayu* and *Vishnu*. In the lists, *Vayu* is sometimes replaced by *Bhavishya*. Although Shiva features in all the Maha Puranas, the primary ones for stories about Shiva and Shiva's lingam are the *Linga, Matsya, Shiva* and *Skanda Purana*s. The stories that follow are an exact reproduction of what is said in the Puranas, mirroring the language used in those texts. These aren't retellings, they are exact tellings.

Jyotirlingam—the Column of Fire

On one occasion, Brahma and Vishnu fought over who was superior, and each thought the other should honour the other first. When they came to blows, their respective mounts also joined in—the swan for Brahma and Garuda for Vishnu. The respective followers also participated on either side. When the clash escalated to the use of divine weapons, there was great danger to the world and the gods prayed to Shiva to intervene. Shiva comforted the gods and told them

---

[7] There are Upa (minor) Puranas, too.

that he would go to the place where Brahma and Vishnu were fighting.

The divine weapons released by Brahma and Vishnu threatened to burn down the world. Between these weapons, Shiva assumed the form of a column of fire. Those divine weapons fell into the column of fire and were pacified. Brahma and Vishnu were amazed. 'What is this extraordinary form? What is this column of fire that has arisen? We must ascertain its top and bottom,' they said. Eager to find out, they decided to do this jointly since neither would be able to do it independently. Vishnu assumed the form of a boar and set out to explore the bottom. Brahma assumed the form of a swan and set out to explore the top. Vishnu penetrated *patala* and went even further down. (Patala is a generic term for the nether regions. But there are seven nether regions: *atala, vitala, nitala, sutala, talatala, rasatala* and *patala*). However, he could not find the foundation of the column, which was as radiant as fire. Exhausted in the form of a boar, Vishnu returned to the former battlefield.

Brahma went up into the sky. He saw a wonderful ketaki flower dislodged from above.[8] It was full of great fragrance and had not faded, even though it had been dislodged many years ago. On witnessing what Brahma and Vishnu were up to, Shiva laughed and when he had shaken his head, the excellent ketaki flower had been dislodged. Brahma asked, 'O flower! Why are you falling? Who wore you?' The ketaki flower replied, 'The top of this column is immeasurable. I

---

[8] The ketaki (*Pandarnus odoratissimus*) flower used to be on Shiva's head until it was cursed.

have been falling for a long time and I have now reached the middle. Therefore, I do not see how you can wish to see the top.' Brahma said, 'In the form of a swan, I have reached this point, and you must do something for me. With me, you must go into Vishnu's presence. Having gone there, you must tell Vishnu that Brahma has seen the end of the column.' This is exactly what happened, and the ketaki flower bore false witness.

Shiva decided to punish the deceitful Brahma and emerged from that lingam made of fire. He bestowed a blessing on Vishnu, ensuring that Vishnu would receive the same reverence as Shiva in this world. As for Brahma, from the middle of his eyebrows, Shiva created a terrible being known as Bhairava. At the time, Brahma possessed five heads. Shiva commanded Bhairava to cut off the head that had uttered those false words. Thus, Brahma came to have only four heads.[9] While Shiva blessed Vishnu so that he would be worshipped with his own sacred places, temples and festivals, he cursed Brahma, saying that nothing of the sort would happen to him. Brahma wouldn't be worshipped. As for the ketaki flower, which had committed an act of perjury, it would never be used in the worship of Shiva.

Brahma and Vishnu worshipped Shiva. ज्योतिः (*jyoti*) means light, radiance, brightness. ज्योतिः + लिंगम् = ज्योतिर्लिंगम् (jyotirlingam).[10] Brahma and Vishnu were the first ones

---

[9] There are other stories about how and why Shiva cut off Brahma's fifth head.

[10] The 'r' appears because of a grammatical rule known as *sandhi*, used when two words are combined.

to worship Shiva in the form of a jyotirlingam. A *tithi* is a lunar day, not identical with a solar day. The tithi, when the jyotirlingam appeared, became famous as Shiva Ratri. Krishna *paksha* is the dark lunar fortnight when the moon wanes. Shukla paksha is the bright lunar fortnight when the moon waxes. And Chaturdashi is the fourteenth lunar tithi. Every Chaturdashi tithi of Krishna paksha is Shiva Ratri (the night of Shiva). Out of these twelve Shiva Ratris, the one in the month of Phalguna (February–March) is special and is known as Maha Shiva Ratri (the great Shiva Ratri). The jyotirlingam appeared on the day of Maha Shiva Ratri. It is also the day when Shiva and Parvati got married. Since there are twelve months, one can understand why there are twelve jyotirlingams.

Human agency alone cannot create a jyotirlingam. Shiva chose to manifest himself as that column of fire. Not even Brahma or Vishnu could have created it. The word स्वयम्भू (*svayambhu*) means someone or something that manifests itself on its own. Every jyotirlingam is a svayambhu lingam, but every svayambhu lingam is not necessarily a jyotirlingam. There are *charalingams* (lingams that move) and acharalingams (lingams that are stationary). ॐ is a *dhvanilingam*. Lingams also exist in the form of yantras and mantras. Since Shiva is everywhere, his lingams are everywhere. The five elements (*bhutas*) are *kshiti* (earth), *apas* (water), *tejas* (fire/energy), *marut* (wind) and *vyom* (space). Accordingly, there are *bhutalingams*. The one made of earth is in Kanchipuram; the one made of water is in Tiruchirappalli; the one made of fire is in Thiruvannamalai;

the one made of wind is in Kalahasti; and the one made of space is in Chidambaram. The one in Thiruvannamalai, made of fire, means the Arunachalesvara temple at the base of Arunachala. According to the Shiva Purana, the place where the jyotirlingam manifested itself during the dispute between Brahma and Vishnu was in Arunachala. There are *rasalingams* made of mercury or gallium. Banasura, with a capital in Shonitpura (today's Tezpur) was one of Shiva's greatest devotees, who worshipped a rasalingam made for him by Vishvakarma, the architect of the devas. The lingams we are usually familiar with are *parthiva* lingams. As the expression implies, parthiva lingams are made of earth, clay or sand. The parthiva lingams found in the river Narmada, also known as *banalingams*, are special because the river originated from Shiva's body and is thus Shiva's daughter. Banalingams are formed through natural processes and are not artificial. In that sense, they are also svayambhu.

The Dvadasha Jyotirlingam Stotram

There are twelve jyotirlingams. The word *dvadasha* means twelve. As mentioned earlier, stotram is a hymn of praise. There are plenty of versions floating around on the net. However, one should be cautious of indiscriminately quoting without checking the source, since these versions frequently make serious grammatical errors. The authentic version is found in the Puranas, with minor variations from one Purana to another.

Somnath

सौराष्ट्रे सोमनाथं च श्रीशैले मल्लिकार्जुनम् । उज्जयिन्यां महाकालमोङ्कारममलेश्वरम् ॥ परल्यां वैद्यनाथं च डाकिन्यां भीमशङ्करम् । सेतुबन्धे तु रामेशं नागेशं दारुकावने ॥ वाराणस्यां तु विश्वेशं त्र्यम्बकं गौतमीतटे । हिमालये तु केदारं घुश्मेशं च शिवालये ॥ एतानि ज्योतिर्लिङ्गानि सायं प्रातः पठेन्नरः । सप्तजन्मकृतं पापं स्मरणेन विनश्यति ॥ एतेषां दर्शनादेव पातकं नैव तिष्ठति । कर्मक्षयो भवेत्तस्य यस्य तुष्टो महेश्वराः ॥

What does this mean?

Somanatha in Sourashtra, Mallikarjuna in Shrishaila;
Mahakala in Ujjayini, Amaleshvara in Omkara.
Vaidyanatha in Parali, Bhimashankara in Dakini; Ramesha

in Setubandha, Nagesha in Darukavana. Vishvesha in Varanasi, Tryambaka on the banks of Goutami; Kedara in Himalaya, Ghushmesha in Shivalaya.

This ends the listing of the twelve. After this,

If a man reads about these jyotrilingams in the morning and evening, as soon as he remembers them, the sins accumulated over seven births are destroyed. If he sees them, it is impossible for sins to remain. If these Maheshvaras are pleased, all his karma is destroyed.

Note that this is the Dvadasha jyotirlingam stotram as stated in the Puranas. Adi Shankaracharya also composed a more elaborate version, which includes descriptions of the twelve jyotirlingams. To illustrate, this is what Adi Shankaracharya had to say about Rameshvara:

सुताम्रपर्णीजलराशियोगे निबध्य सेतुं विशिखैरसंख्यैः । श्रीरामचन्द्रेण समर्पितं तं रामेश्वराख्यं नियतं नमामि ॥

I control myself and prostrate myself before the one named Rameshvara. Shri Ramachandra worshipped this. He used innumerable arrows and constructed a bridge at the confluence of the mass of waters of the excellent Tamraparni.

To repeat, this is not part of the core Dvadasha jyotirlingam stotram.

For most, there is no dispute about where they are geographically located. For three, the geographical identification is not that robust. In the famous jyotirlingam stotram, the first jyotirlingam is Somanatha, in Sourashtra.

There is a story connected with every jyotirlingam, typically, about a parthiva lingam turning into a jyotirlingam as a result of a boon granted by Shiva. We will come to those stories later. There is no subjectivity about deciding where Sourashtra is. The next one is Mallikarjuna, in Shrishaila, with no geographical problem whatsoever. Mahakala in Ujjayini (Ujjain) is obvious too. Omkara, or Amaleshvara (also written as Amareshvara), is different. Omkareshwara is in Madhya Pradesh, on the banks of the Narmada. Those who have been to Omkareshwara will have noticed there are two lingams there—and Amareshvara (also known as Amaleshvara) on the bank.

Which is the true jyotirlingam? Both are jyotirlingams. By the way, the island is in the shape of oum, or aum, which is how we get the name of Omkareshwara. The island is named Mandhata because the sage Mandhata worshipped Shiva there. Given today's geography, there can be no issue with Vaidyanatha, though one doesn't know what to make of the expression *parali*. Bhimashankara is in Dakini.

Omkareshwara

Omkareshwara

Most people will identify Bhimashankara as the one in Maharashtra, near Pune, but Dakini is not a neat geographical place either. We will see from the subsequent account that Bhimashankara might very well have been in the Kamarupa region. There can be no confusion about Rameshvara where the bridge was built. The jyotirlingam of, and it is not easy to identify where it is located geographically. While Darukavana is usually understood to be a forest of devadaru trees, in this story, the name owes its origin to a demon named Daruka. Everyone knows where Varanasi is. Tryambakeshvara is easy to identify on the banks of Goutami (another name for Godavari). Kedara, in the Himalayas, causes no problems. This leaves Ghushmesha. Shivalaya means Shiva's abode,

Bhimashankara

43

and it can be anywhere. Today, we have certainly identified geographical locations with the twelve jyotirlingams, but due to the reasons mentioned, three of the identifications are somewhat suspect.

Let us now turn to the stories.

Somanatha in Sourashtra

Soma means the moon, also known as Chandra or Indu. Somanatha means Soma's lord.

Daksha had twenty-seven daughters. These are the twenty-seven nakshatras. He bestowed them on Chandra. (In standard accounts, Daksha had forty daughters, and he bestowed the remaining daughters on the twin Ashvins and others.) Obtaining Chandra as their husband, the twenty-seven nakshatras became especially radiant. Having obtained them, Chandra also shone all the time. A jewel shines even more when set in gold, and gold also dazzles more with a jewel. Among all his wives, he loved the one known as Rohini (Aldebaran) the most. The others weren't loved that much. As a result, they were miserable, so they sought refuge with their father. They went to him and reported their miseries. Hearing this, Daksha also grieved. He went to Chandra and addressed him in conciliatory words. Daksha said, 'You have been born into a sparkling lineage. If you have been discriminated against, you should not do it again. It is said that such differentiation in conduct leads to hell.' Daksha requested Chandra, his son-in-law. Deluded, Chandra did not follow his words. Attached to Rohini, he did not pay attention to the others. Daksha knew about good policy. Hearing this, Daksha was filled with sorrow and went to Chandra again. Daksha said, 'O Chandra! Listen. I have already asked you repeatedly. But since you did not pay any attention, you will suffer from consumption.' As soon as he said this, Chandra suffered from consumption. When the moon started to decay, there were great sounds of lamentation. All the devas and rishis wondered, 'What should be done now? What will happen?'

Chandra told Indra and the other gods everything, who, with Vasishta and the other rishis, sought refuge with Brahma. They told him everything. Brahma said,

Alas! A great misery has arisen for all the world. Chandra has always been wicked, and Daksha has cursed him now. Chandra has engaged in many kinds of wicked conduct. But describing them afresh serves no purpose. Why does he keep doing such things? What has happened, has happened. It is certainly the case that it cannot be reversed. Therefore, listen. Along with devas, let Chandra go to the auspicious *kshetra*[11] of Prabhasa (near Dvaraka). Let him follow the norms and use the Mahamrityunjaya Mantra to worship Shiva.

(ॐ त्र्यम्बकं यजामहे सुगन्धिं पुष्टिवर्धनम् । उर्वारुकमिव बन्धनान्मृत्योर्मुक्षीय मामृतात् ॥) (We worship the fragrant Tryambaka, who

---

[11] Literally, *kshetra* means field and is an auspicious place of pilgrimage. *Tirtha* is often used as a synonymous word. But, in a *tirtha*, a person descends into flowing water. There is no such nuance for *kshetra*.

enhances our nourishment. Like cucumbers are severed from their bonds, let me be separated from death, but not from immortality.) In front of Isha, let Chandra constantly torment himself through austerities. If Shiva is pleased, he will remove his consumption.

Hearing Brahma's words, the gods and rishis returned to the place where Daksha and the moon were. Assuring Daksha, all the gods and rishis took Chandra and went to Prabhasa. Following the norms, they instated a parthiva lingam and used the Mahamrityunjaya Mantra to worship it. Having ensured that Chandra was going to undertake the worship, the devas and rishis returned to their own homes.

For six months, Chandra constantly tormented himself through austerities. He used the Mahamrityunjaya Mantra to worship Vrishadhvaja.[12] The moon chanted the mantra a million times. He used the Mahamrityunjaya Mantra to perform *dhyana*.[13] Beholding this, Shankara was pleased. He is affectionate towards his devotees. The lord manifested himself before his devotee and said, 'Ask for a boon, whatever your mind desires. O moon! I am pleased with you.' Chandra replied, 'O lord of devas! If you are pleased, what can I not accomplish? O Shankara! Nonetheless, please counter the consumption in my body. Please pardon everything else I have done, and please always do what is beneficial for me.' Thus addressed, Shiva said, 'O Chandra! For one fortnight, every day, you will decline by one digit. In another fortnight,

[12] Shiva's name, since he has a bull on his banner.
[13] Meditation, one of the eight limbs of *yoga*.

you will constantly increase by one digit.' At this, the devas and rishis assembled again, delighted. They prayed to Shiva, 'O Shambhu! Along with Uma, please remain immobile in this spot.' In those ancient times, Chandra devoutly praised Shankara. To increase the greatness of the kshetra and enhance Chandra's fame, Shankara remained in the place named after Chandra. It became famous in the three worlds under the name of Someshvara. People who worship there can destroy diseases like consumption and leprosy. There is a pond there, established by all the devas and subsequently divided among themselves by Shiva and Brahma. This destroys all sins and is famous on earth as Chandrakunda. A man who bathes there is freed from all sins. This is how, through Chandra's prayers and austerities, there came to be a jyotirlingam in Somanatha.

Mallikarjuna in Shrishaila

Shrishaila

Shiva and Parvati have two sons, Kumara, or Kartikeya, and Ganesha, or Vinayaka. Most accounts, though not always, describe Kumara as the elder of the two. When the sons grew up, it was time for them to get married. Who would be married first, Kumara or Ganesha? The parents decided to have a competition. Whoever would go around the world seven times first would be married first. Kumara dashed off on his mount, the peacock. Ganesha's mount was the slower mouse. Being on the portly side, he was not as swift and spirited as Kumara. Ganesha knew he stood no chance, so he decided to circle his parents seven times. His parents were the world. Therefore, circumambulating them was like circumambulating the world. This was impeccable logic, one that Shiva and Parvati couldn't counter. Therefore, much before Kumara returned from his travels, Ganesha was married off to Riddhi and Siddhi.

Devarshi Narada, though a divine sage, is fond of creating conflict and dissension. When Kumara returned to Kailasa, Narada promptly went and told him everything about Ganesha's marriage. Kumara's mind was in a whirl. His younger brother had married before him. Hearing this, Kumara prostrated himself before his parents. Though his parents tried to restrain him, he went to Mount Krauncha and resolved never to marry.

Separated from Kumara, his mother was miserable. However, Shambhu spoke to her and made her understand. 'O Parvati! Who are you grieving? Your son will return. Give up this terrible sorrow.' But, suffering from great grief, Parvati did not pay any attention to this. Therefore, Shankara sent the devas and rishis. All the devas and rishis went, along with their followers. They went there to bring back Kumara. However, Kumara did not pay heed to the prayers of the devas or Shiva's command. As a result of their love, Shiva and Parvati went to the place where their son was. Knowing that they had come and feeling no love for them, Kumara went far away from Mount Krauncha. But they remained there, in forms full of energy. Out of affection for their son, Shiva and Parvati go there on every auspicious day. They go there to see their son, Kumara. Shiva himself goes there on *amavasya* (the night of the new moon), and Parvati goes there on the day of *purnima* (the night of the full moon). This is how Shiva's lingam of Mallikarjuna originated. Shiva is there as Arjuna, and Parvati is there as Mallika.

Mahakala in Ujjayini

Ujjayini (Ujjain) is an ancient city. It had other names too, such as Avanti and Vishala. There is more than one story about Mahakala.

A Brahmana, auspicious in deeds, lived in Avanti. He always studied and performed rites from the Vedas. He maintained the sacrificial fire and always worshipped Shiva. Every day, the Brahmana worshipped a parthiva image. The Brahmana, Vedapriya, obtained the fruits of all the rites. He attained proper *jnana* (knowledge), which is the ultimate goal for the virtuous. He had four sons who were just like him. Their constantly devotion to worshipping Shiva ensured that they were not inferior to their father. These sons were

Devapriya, Priyamedha, Sukrita and Dharmavahi. As a consequence of the power of their good merits, happiness increased on earth—just as the moon constantly waxes during Shukla paksha, their good qualities flourished and brought happiness.

On Mount Ratnamala, there was a great asura named Dushana. The king of daityas was powerful, and he constantly harmed the cause of dharma. Thanks to a boon obtained from Brahma, he regarded the world as insignificant. He defeated the devas, ousting them from their positions. Like a lion destroying hares, the wicked one shattered the dharma of the Vedas and the dharma of the Smriti texts everywhere on earth. 'However, it can still be seen in that solitary and beautiful city of Avanti.' With this thought, Dushana, the great asura, surrounded himself with many soldiers. He went there, intending to destroy all the Brahmanas who were there. Having reached there, the immensely crooked one, who hated Brahmanas, addressed the daityas in these words. He said,

> Why don't the wicked Brahmanas act in accordance with my words? It is my view that all those who follow the dharma of the Vedas must be punished. I have defeated all the devas and kings in the world. Are we incapable of bringing Brahmanas under our control? If they wish to remain alive and obtain a share in happiness, let them give up Shiva's dharma and the supreme dharma of the Vedas. Otherwise, there will be doubt about their remaining alive.

When this was decided, four daityas surrounded the city from four directions, resembling fires that arise at the time of dissolution. The Brahmanas heard about the attempts made by the daityas. However, devoted to performing dhyana on Shiva, they were not saddened at all. The Brahmanas resorted to their fortitude and did not deviate the least bit from their supreme dhyana. If Shiva is before you, who can suffer? Meanwhile, that auspicious city was overwhelmed. The suffering people went and sought refuge with the Brahmanas. The people exclaimed, 'What is to be done? The wicked ones have arrived. They have caused violence to many people and are approaching close.' Hearing their words, the Brahmanas, who were the sons of Vedapriya and who always placed their trust in Shankara, replied. The Brahmanas said,

> We do not possess an army that can cause fear among the wicked. We do not have weapons that can be used to drive them back. This general dishonour also reflects on the one who is our refuge. Who is capable of acting against Shiva? The Lord Shiva will protect us from the fear caused by the asuras. There is no other refuge in the world. Shiva is affectionate towards his devotees.

They worshipped the parthiva lingam. Having done this, the Brahmanas immersed themselves in dhyana.

The daitya and his soldiers saw the Brahmanas. Dushana said, 'Kill them. Bind them.' However, the Brahmanas, who were the sons of Devapriya, were devoted to the path of performing dhyana on Shambhu.

They did not hear the words uttered by the daitya. The evil-souled one wished to kill the Brahmanas. But before he could do so, the place where the parthiva lingam was placed sank into a pit, making a loud sound. Shiva arose from within that pit, assuming a hideous form. He became famous as Mahakala, the one who slays the wicked and is the destination of the virtuous. He said, 'I am Mahakala, who rises against wicked ones like you. O crooked ones! Leave. Go far away from these Brahmanas.' Saying this, Mahakala Shankara uttered the sound of *humkara*[14] and instantly reduced Dushana and his army to ashes. Some soldiers were killed. Some other soldiers ran away. Dushana was killed by Shiva, the paramatman. Darkness is destroyed when it sees the sun. Like that, upon seeing Shiva, the soldiers were destroyed. The drums of the devas were sounded, and flowers were showered. All the devas, Vishnu, Brahma and the others assembled. They devotedly prostrated themselves before the divinity Shankara, who brings welfare to the world. They joined hands in salutation and praised him with many kinds of hymns. Pleased, Shiva himself comforted the Brahmanas. Mahakala Maheshvara said, 'Ask for a boon.' Hearing this, all the Brahmanas joined hands in salutation. Full of devotion towards Shiva, they prostrated themselves, lowered their heads and spoke. Brahmanas said, 'O Mahakala! O Mahadeva! O chastiser of the wicked! O Shambhu! O Shiva! Please grant us

---

[14] *Humkara* is the sound '*hum*', which carries special mystical powers.

liberation from this ocean of *samsara*.[15] For the protection of the world, please remain established here. Always save those who see you.' Thus addressed, Shiva remained in that beautiful pit, so that he might save devotees and grant them a virtuous destination. From his form as a lingam, Shiva's region extends for one *krosha* in each of the four directions.[16] Under the name of Mahakaleshvara, Shiva is famous around the world.

Mahakaleshwar

---

[15] The worldly cycle of death and rebirth.

[16] Krosha is a measure of distance. It is the distance at which one can hear a shout. Four kroshas make one yojana. A yojana is the distance that can be travelled in a single yoking and is between eight and nine miles.

There is yet another story about Mahakala. There was a great king in Ujjayini, known by the name of Chandrasena. He knew the truth about all the sacred texts. He had conquered his senses and was Shiva's devotee. The *gana* Manibhadra was the king's friend.[17] He was foremost among Girisha's ganas and revered by all the worlds. On one occasion, Manibhadra was pleased with him and gave him the great jewel Chintamani. This jewel was as radiant as *koustubha*,[18] and its resplendence was like that of the sun. If one meditated on it, saw it or heard about it, it was certain to bring auspiciousness. If brass, copper, tin, stone or other objects touched its shining surface, they immediately turned into gold. With Shiva as his refuge and the dazzling Chintamani around his neck, King Chandrasena was as resplendent as Surya amidst the devas. Upon hearing that the supreme king Chandrasena had the Chinatamani around his neck, the hearts of all the other kings on earth were agitated by their greed. They were all jealous of Chandrasena and the jewel that he obtained from a divine source, and they used their intelligence to devise various means of taking it from him. Even though all the kings asked Chandrasena for his jewel, he remained firm in his devotion to Mahakala and repulsed them. The kings from all those countries became angry and assembled four kinds

---

[17] A gana is Shiva's attendant and companion. A leader of ganas is ganeshvara or ganapati. There were many ganeshvaras or ganapatis. The one we know as Vinayaka was one of them, but not the only one. Nandi was also a ganeshvara.

[18] The jewel Vishnu wears on his chest.

of forces.[19] They made attempts to defeat Chandrasena in a battle. With many soldiers, they laid siege to the four gates of Ujjayini. When Chandrasena saw that all the kings had laid siege to his city, he sought refuge with Mahakaleshvara. He didn't eat; he was firm in his determination that there was no other option. Single-mindedly, he worshipped Mahakala day and night. Bhagavan Mahakala Shambhu was pleased and devised a means to protect him.

Mahakaleshwar

At that time, there was a *gopi*[20] in that excellent city. She wandered around and approached Mahakala, bringing her

---

[19] Horses, elephants, chariots and infantry.

[20] A gopa is a cowherd; gopi is the feminine.

child with her. She had been carrying her five-year-old child by herself, as her husband was dead. She saw the king worship Mahakala with a lot of love. She witnessed the worship of Shiva in an incredible and wonderful manner. Prostrating herself, she returned to her own tent. The gopi's son witnessed everything, full of curiosity. He made up his mind to worship Shiva, too. He brought a stone and placed it in a vacant spot near the tent. It was not far from his own tent, and devotedly, he regarded this as his own Shiva lingam. He thought of artificial fragrances, ornaments, garments, incense, lamps, *akshata* (unhusked grain) and *naivedya* (divine offering). He repeatedly performed the worship with beautiful flowers and leaves. He danced in different kinds of ways and repeatedly prostrated himself. At such a time, when the son's mind was fixed on Shiva, the gopi lovingly called him to have his food. Despite being called several times, the child's mind was fixed on worshipping Shiva. He did not wish to eat. She went there and saw him seated in front of Shiva with his eyes closed. She struck him angrily and dragged him by the hand. Though he was struck and dragged, the child did not leave. Therefore, she destroyed the worship and flung the lingam far away. When she did this, her son lamented and reprimanded her. The gopi entered her own house again, full of rage. Seeing that his mother had destroyed the worship of the divinity who wields the trident, the child fell to the ground and lamented, 'O Lord! O divinity!' Overcome by grief, he lost his senses. He regained his senses after a while and opened his eyes. The child saw that the tent was transformed into Mahakala's beautiful temple as a result of Shiva's favours.

There were large doors made of gold; there were broad and excellent gates; there was an extremely expensive and radiant altar, made of sparkling blue diamonds; there were many wonderful pots made of molten gold; there were shining pillars encrusted with gems; the floor was made of slabs of crystal; and right in the middle, there was a bejewelled lingam of Shankara, the ocean of compassion. The gopi's son saw that the objects he had used for the worship were also there. Seeing this, the child was amazed, and he instantly stood up. It was as if he was immersed in an ocean of supreme bliss. He repeatedly praised Girisha and prostrated himself before him. When the sun set, the child emerged from Shiva's temple. He saw that his own tent had come to resemble Indra's city. It had suddenly been converted into one that was made of gold. It was wonderful and immensely radiant. He entered his house, which was filled with everything beautiful. It was strewn with a large number of jewels and a lot of gold. He rejoiced. The night was about to start. He saw his mother there, resembling a celestial woman with all the divine signs. Her limbs were radiant, decorated with bejewelled ornaments. She seemed to be a celestial lady. The son, the recipient of Shiva's favours, was full of joy and quickly woke his mother up. Waking up, she saw these wonders, the likes of which had not been seen before. Immersed in great joy, she embraced her son.

She heard everything from her son's mouth to the effect that all this was because of Shiva's favours. She sent word to the king, who was constantly worshipping Shiva. After completing the rituals of the night, the king quickly arrived there. He saw the powers of the gopi's son, as a result of satisfying Shiva. The lord of the earth and all the advisers and the purohita saw this. They were immersed in an ocean of supreme bliss. King Chandrasena's eyes shed tears of love. Rejoicing, he chanted Shiva's name and embraced the child. There were great and wonderful festivities. All of them were overwhelmed with joy and chanted about Mahesha. Witnessing Shiva's greatness and this wonderful incident, the citizens were filled with respect and the night passed as if it were only an instant. In the morning, the kings, who had laid siege to the city in order to fight, heard through their spies what had happened. All those kings assembled and, scared by what they had heard, they spoke to each other:

This king, Chandrasena, is Shiva's devotee and is impossible to defeat. The lord Mahakala is favourably disposed towards the city of Ujjayini. He is Shiva's devotee, and even the children of the city follow Shiva's *vrata*s (vows). King Chandrasena is Shankara's great devotee. It is clear that if we oppose him, Shiva will be angry. His rage will bring destruction to all of us. Therefore, we must have an alliance with the king. If we do this, Mahesha will show us his compassion.

Having decided this, the kings gave up their wicked enmity. Delighted, all of them cast aside the weapons in their hands. With King Chandrasena's permission, they entered the beautiful city, protected by Mahakala. They happily worshipped Mahakala. The kings also went to the gopi's house. All of them praised the advent of her divine good fortune. Chandrasena welcomed them and honoured them. He was seated on an expensive seat; amazed, they honoured him back. They saw the Shiva lingam and Shiva's temple, which had manifested because of the favours of the gopi's son. Their minds turned completely towards Shiva. All the kings were delighted with the gopi's son. Desiring Shiva's compassion, they gave him many objects.

Mahakaleshwar

At this time, worshipped by all the residents of heaven, the energetic Hanuman, the lord of *vanaras* (forest-dwellers), manifested himself there. On his arrival, the kings were filled with reverence. They stood up and bent down, images of humility and devotion. Worshipped, the lord of monkeys sat down in their midst. He embraced the gopi's son. He glanced towards the kings and spoke:

O fortunate kings and all those who have bodies! Listen. For those with bodies, there is no destination other than Shiva. It is good fortune that the gopi's son witnessed Shiva's worship. Even if one worships Shiva without mantras, Shiva can be reached. He is supreme among Shambhu's devotees and has enhanced the fame of the lineage of gopas. He will enjoy all the objects of pleasure in this world. After the period of enjoyment is over, he will obtain emancipation. In the eighth generation of his lineage, there will be an immensely illustrious one named Nanda. As his son, he will obtain Krishna, who will be Narayana himself. From now on, this son of a gopa will be famous in the world and will be addressed by the name of Shrikara.

These are the stories about Mahakala.

Amareshvara in Omkara

On some occasions, the illustrious sage Narada went to Shiva in the place known as Gokarna. With great devotion, the supreme sage went to Vindhya, the lord of mountains. The mountain worshipped him with a great deal of respect. It stationed itself in front of Narada and said, 'Everything exists in me. There is nothing that does not exist in me.'

Narada heard Vindhya's words, which were full of sentiments of pride. The destroyer of pride sighed and remained there. Vindhya asked, 'Why have you sighed? What do you see lacking in me?' Hearing this, Narada, the great sage, replied, 'Everything exists in you. But Meru is loftier than you. It is classified as a deva, but you never are.' Saying this, Narada went away. Vindhya lamented, 'Shame on my life. I will perform austerities and worship Vishveshvara Shambhu.' Having made up its mind, it sought refuge with Shankara. It happily went to the place known as Omkara. It fashioned Shiva's parthiva image there. For six months, it constantly worshipped Shambhu. Devoted to dhyana on Shiva, it did not move from the place where it was performing austerities. Seeing that Vindhya had tormented itself in this way, Shiva was pleased. He displayed his own form, which was difficult for even yogis to see. He said, 'I am pleased. Tell me, what is on your mind? I am pleased with your austerities. I grant devotees what they desire.' Vindhya replied, 'O lord of devas! If you are pleased with me, please grant me intelligence so that I can be successful in my desired task. You are always affectionate towards your devotees.' Hearing this, Bhagavan Shambhu thought about it for some time. 'Vindhya is foolish in intelligence and desires this boon so that it can oppress others. What will I do? I must bestow a boon that brings auspiciousness. The bestowal of a boon must not lead to great hardship for others.' Nevertheless, Shambhu bestowed that excellent boon. 'O Vindhya, king of mountains! Do whatever you wish.' At that time, devas and rishis, the stores of purity, worshipped Shankara and said, 'Please remain in this spot.' Hearing the words of the devas, Parameshvara was pleased. Delighted, he wished to be the reason for happiness in the world. The single lingam of Omkara is divided into two. In Pranava (that is, in the place in the shape of Pranava), Sadashiva is known under the name of Omkara. Parameshvara also exists in parthiva form.[21] Both grant devotees what they desire. Both bestow objects of pleasure and emancipation. Devas and rishis worshipped him. Having satisfied Vrishadhvaja, they obtained many boons. Vindhya became happier at having accomplished its own task and gave up its lamentation.

Vaidyanatha in Parali

Ravana was the best among the rakshasas, and he was respected. He worshipped Hara on Kailasa, the supreme among mountains. Though the worship continued for a long time, Hara was not pleased. To please Shiva, he then embarked on other austerities. On the slopes of Mount Himalaya, there is a spot known for bestowing *siddhi*.[22] This is set amidst a clump of trees facing south. The prosperous Poulastya Ravana[23] dug a pit in the ground and established a sacrificial fire there. He instated Shiva near this and offered

---

[21] A gopa is a cowherd; gopi is the feminine.

[22] The word *siddhi* has several meanings. In a generic sense, it means success in attaining an objective. In a narrower sense, it means specific powers.

[23] Ravana was the son of Vishrava, who was the son of Poulastya.

oblations into the fire. In the summer, he stationed himself in the middle of five fires.[24] During the monsoon, he slept on the bare ground. In winter, he remained in the water. Despite his many austerities, Mahesha, the *paramatman*, was not pleased. Evil-souled ones find it difficult to worship him. The great-souled Ravana, the lord of the daityas, then started to slice off his heads and use them to worship Shankara. As he severed each head, he followed the norms and worshipped Shiva. In this way, in due order, he cut off nine heads. When only one head was left, Shankara was pleased. Affectionate towards his devotees, he was satisfied and manifested himself. The Lord healed the heads that had been severed earlier. He granted his wish of supreme and unmatched strength. Ravana, the rakshasa, thus obtained his favours.[25]

Ravana joined his hands in salutation and spoke to Shiva Shambhu. He said, 'O lord of the devas! If you are pleased with me, I will take you to Lanka. Please make my wish come true.' When Shambhu was addressed by Ravana in this way, he was faced with great difficulty. His mind wavering, Shiva said, 'O best among rakshasas! With great devotion, take my excellent lingam to your own house. However, if you place the lingam down on the ground, it will remain stationary in that spot.' Ravana agreed to this and, taking the lingam

---

[24] Four fires on four sides and the sun overhead.

[25] Vaidya is a physician. Since Shiva healed Ravana, he is known as Vaidyanatheshvara. The stotram Ravana used to worship Shiva is known as the *Shiva Tandava Stotram*.

with him, proceeded towards his own residence. As a result of Shiva's maya, he felt like passing urine along the way. Lord Ravana, born in the Poulastya lineage, was incapable of resisting this. He saw a gopa there and requested that he hold the lingam.[26] After some time, oppressed by the weight, the gopa placed it down on the ground. The lingam was made of the essence of the *vajra*[27] and remained stationary there. It yields everything desired. If one sees it, all sins are destroyed. This lingam is named Vaidyanatheshvara. It is famous in the three worlds and bestows objects of pleasure and emancipation on the virtuous. For the welfare of all the worlds, that lingam remained stationary there. Having obtained a great and excellent boon, Ravana returned to his own residence.

Having obtained the great and excellent boon, Ravana returned home. Hearing this, all the devas, Indra and the others, and the sages became anxious and spoke to each other. The devas and others said, 'The evil-souled Ravana hates devas. He is crooked and wickedly intelligent. Having obtained a boon from Shiva, he will inflict misery on us. What will we do? What will happen next?' Dejected, they invited Narada and asked him. The devas said, 'O supreme sage! You are capable of accomplishing every task. Devise a way to free the devas of their misery. Ravana is extremely wicked. What will he not do?' Narada replied, 'O devas! I

---

[26] In some stories, this is Ganesha disguised as a boy.

[27] *Vajra* is the name of Indra's weapon. The word also means a diamond.

will do what is needed.' Saying this, the devarshi went to Ravana's abode.

When he reached there, he was honoured with every kind of welcome and spoke affectionately. Narada said, 'O supreme among rakshasas! You are blessed. You are a noble devotee of Shiva's, intent on austerities. Tell me everything about what you did and how you worshipped Shiva.' Ravana answered,

O great sage! I went to Kailasa to undertake austerities. There, I tormented myself through terrible austerities for a very long period. When Shankara was not pleased, I returned to a clump of trees and performed austerities again. In the summer, I was in the middle of five fires. During the monsoon, I slept on the bare ground. In winter, I remained inside the water. But even then, Shankara was not pleased with me. As a result of this, I became angry and dug a pit in the ground. I instated a sacrificial fire there and fashioned a parthiva lingam. Following the norms, I worshipped Shambhu with fragrances, sandalwood, incense and many kinds of naivedya. To please Shankara, I prostrated myself and used sacred hymns, singing, dancing, the playing of musical instruments and the symbolic offering of my mouth and fingers. I used these and many other means sanctioned by the sacred texts to worship Bhagavan Hara. But even then, Bhagavan Hara was not satisfied and did not manifest himself in front of me. Since my austerities were unsuccessful, I was dejected. 'Shame on my body and strength. Shame on my efforts at austerities.' Saying this, I offered many oblations into the fire that had been instated. Then I thought, 'I will offer my own body into the fire.' I severed my heads and offered them to that purifying blaze. I severed them one by one and purified them in this way. I offered nine such heads to Shankara. When I was about to sever the tenth head, Hara himself appeared before me, in the form of a mass of radiance. Affectionate towards his devotees and delighted, he immediately spoke to me. 'I am pleased. Tell me. I will give you the boon that your mind wishes for.' Full of great devotion, I clasped my hands, prostrated myself and praised him. I said, 'O lord of devas! If you are pleased, what cannot be achieved by me? If this is the case, please grant me unmatched strength.' When Shiva is satisfied and full of compassion, he bestows everything. He spoke words of assent, granting me what my mind wished for. His favourable glance is invincible and superior to the best of *vaidyas* (physicians). When the paramatman looked at me, my head was affixed again. In this way, my body became just what it had been earlier. Through his favours, I obtained all these fruits. As requested by me, Vrishadhvaja remained there. He is named Vaidyanatheshvara and is famous in the three worlds. Maheshvara is in the form of the jyotirlingam, and if one sees him or worships him, one obtains objects of pleasure and emancipation. He brings welfare to all of the world. Specifically, I worshipped that jyotirlingam. Having prostrated myself, I returned to conquer the three worlds.

Hearing his words, devarshi was alarmed.

However, laughing in his mind, Narada spoke to Ravana. Narada said,

O best among rakshasas! I will tell you something that is beneficial for you. You just told me that Shiva bestowed all this on you for your welfare. But you should never accept what he said to be true. When he is in one of his aberrations, there is nothing he does not say. It may not be true. You are dear to me. How will one know it is true? For your own welfare, you should again go there and do the following: You should make an effort to raise Kailasa. If you are able to raise Kailasa, then there is no doubt that you have been successful in every possible way. Set it back where it was and happily return.

Deluded by destiny, Ravana took these words to be beneficial for him. Taking the sage's words to be true, he went to Kailasa. Having gone there, he raised the mountain. Everyone on the mountain suffered a catastrophe and fell over each other. Seeing this, Girisha asked, 'What is this?' Parvati laughed and replied to Shambhu, 'These are the fruits of having a good disciple. This is indeed a true disciple. Such unmatched strength has been bestowed on an excellent hero, possessing a serene atman.' Maheshvara heard Parvati's words, which were laced with sarcasm. He thought that Ravana was ungrateful and insolent because of his strength. Therefore, he cursed him. Mahadeva said, 'O Ravana! You are an evil devotee. You are evil-minded. Give up the insolence you possess. Soon, there will be a person who will rob your hands of their insolence.' Narada heard everything that happened there. However, Ravana was also pleased in his mind and returned to his residence. Deluded by his strength, he was now supremely confident. As a result of Shiva's command, he obtained great energy and divine weapons. There was no warrior who could counter Ravana in a clash. Eventually, Ravana was killed by Rama.

Bhimashankara in Dakini

Bhimashankara

In the region known as Kamarupa, to ensure the welfare of the worlds and make people the recipients of fortune and happiness, Shankara himself took an avatara. Earlier, there was an immensely valiant rakshasa named Bhima. He caused misery to all beings and continuously destroyed dharma. He was the exceptionally strong son of Kumbhakarna and Karkati. When Kumbhakarna, who caused terror to the worlds, was killed by Rama, along with his mother, Bhima resided on Mount Sahya. Along with her son, the rakshasi also resided on Sahya. Bhima was crooked and terrible in character. He caused misery in the worlds. On one occasion, while still a child, he questioned his mother, Karkati. Bhima asked, 'O mother! Who is my father? Where is he? Why are you alone here? I wish to know everything. Please tell me the truth now.' Thus, asked by her son, the wicked rakshasi replied,

Your father was Kumbhakarna, Ravana's younger brother. The immensely strong Rama killed him and his brother. On one occasion, the rakshasa Kumbhakarna came here. O son! In those earlier times, he forcibly enjoyed me. The immensely strong one left me here and went to Lanka. I have not seen Lanka. I have resided here. My father's name was Karkata, and my mother was known as Pushkashi. My husband was Viradha, killed by Rama earlier. When my beloved husband was killed, I remained with my parents. My parents are now dead. A rishi reduced them to ashes. The great-souled Sutikshna was Agastya's disciple. When they went there to devour him, he used his excellent austerities to destroy them. Since that earlier occasion, I have resided on this mountain, miserable and alone. I lived here, afflicted by grief. I was without support and refuge. At that time, the rakshasa, who was Ravana's younger brother, arrived here. He had intercourse with me. Leaving me, he went away. After that, you, the immensely strong and valiant one, were born. Having obtained support again, I spent my time.

Hearing these words, Bhima, terrible in valour, was enraged. He thought, 'What will I do against Hari? He has killed my father and my maternal grandfather. He killed Viradha and caused many kinds of misery. If I am a true son, I will make Hari suffer.' Having made up his mind, Bhima left to torment himself through great austerities directed towards Brahma.[28]

With his mind fixed on dhyana, he performed those great austerities for 1000 years. He raised his hands and stood on one foot, fixing his eyes on the sun. Bhima, the son of a rakshasa, remained in that posture. An extremely terrible energy rose from his head. Scorched by this, the devas sought refuge with Brahma. They devotedly prostrated themselves before the Creator and used many kinds of hymns to praise him. All of them, including Indra, informed him about their miseries. The devas said, 'O Brahma! Because of the rakshasa's energy, the world is about to suffer. O Vidhatri! In truth, please grant the wicked one the boon he desires. Otherwise, all of us will be burnt down by his fierce energy. Therefore,

---

[28] We should note the references to both Sahya and Kamarupa, confusing the geographical identification.

please grant him what he wishes for and save all of us from destruction.' Hearing their words, Brahma, the grandfather of the worlds, went there to grant him a boon. He addressed him with these words. Brahma said, 'I am pleased. Ask for the boon that is in your mind.' Hearing Vidhatri's words, the rakshasa replied, 'O lord of devas! O one who is seated on a lotus! If you are pleased and if you wish to grant me a boon, please grant me unmatched strength.' Saying this, the rakshasa prostrated himself before Brahma, who granted him the boon. Having obtained unmatched strength from Brahma, the rakshasa returned home.

Bhima prostrated himself before his mother and proudly said, 'O mother! Behold my strength now. I will cause great carnage among the devas, headed by Indra, even if Hari helps them.' Saying this, Bhima first defeated the devas, along with Indra. Terrible in his valour, he ousted them from their positions and occupied those positions. When the immortals requested Hari, he also defeated him in a battle. Delighted, the daitya then started to conquer the earth. He first went to defeat Sudakshina, the lord and king of Kamarupa. There was an extremely terrible battle between the two. As a result of Brahma's powers and the strength of the boon, the asura, terrible in his valour, defeated the great and extremely valiant king of Kamarupa. The king was Shiva's servant. He was extremely devoted to dharma and was loved by Hara. Nevertheless, the wicked Bhima seized him, bound him in chains and imprisoned him in solitary confinement. He seized his entire kingdom and everything it allied to. There, the king created an excellent parthiva image.

Desiring welfare, he started to worship Shiva. In his mind, he invoked Ganga through many means to perform bathing and other rites required for Shankara's worship. Following the norms decreed for a parthiva image, the excellent king undertook dhyana and other rites. He prostrated himself, used the mudras and an asana and chanted hymns. He happily did everything required to worship Shankara. He used his knowledge to perform japa with the Panchakshara Mantra, prefixed with Pranava.[29] He did not find the time to do anything else. His wife was a virtuous lady named Dakshina. The king's beloved also happily worshipped a parthiva image. The couple was single-minded in their worship of Shankara, who ensures the welfare of devotees. They were constantly engaged in the worship of Shiva.

The rakshasa was deluded because of the boon and his insolence. He destroyed sacrifices and rites and said, 'Let everything be given to me.' With many soldiers who were evil-souled rakshasas, he brought the entire earth under his control. He destroyed the dharma of the Vedas, the dharma of the sacred texts, the dharma of the Smriti texts and the dharma of the Puranas. He conquered and enjoyed everything on his own. The devas, along with Indra, and the rishis suffered. Extremely miserable, the Brahmanas were expelled from the world. Along with Indra, all the devas and rishis were incapacitated. With Brahma and Vishnu leading them, they went and sought refuge with Shankara.

---

[29] Pranava is oum, japa is silent chanting, asana is a physical posture, and mudra is a posture for the hands.

They praised Shankara, who brings welfare to the worlds, with many kinds of hymns. Along the auspicious banks of the River Mahakoshi, they pleased him. They created a parthiva image and, following the norms, worshipped it. In due order, they praised him with many kinds of hymns and prostrated themselves. In this way, the devas used hymns to praise Shambhu. Pleased, he addressed the gods with these words. Shiva said, 'O Hari! O Vidhatri! O devas! O all the rishis! I am pleased with you. Ask for a boon. What do I have to do for you?' The devas clasped their hands, prostrated themselves and spoke to Shiva,

O lord of the devas! You know everything. You are established in the mind of every person. You are inside everyone, and there is nothing that is not known to you. O protector! Nevertheless, listen. Following your command, we will tell you about our misery. O Mahadeva! Please cast a glance of compassion towards us. There is a powerful rakshasa, the son of Karkati and Kumbhakarna. As the result of a boon he has obtained from Brahma, he constantly oppresses devas. Please slay the rakshasa named Bhima, who is causing this misery. O Mahesha! O Lord! Please show us your compassion. Please do not delay.

All the gods spoke in this way to Shambhu, who is affectionate towards his devotees. He told the devas, 'I will kill him.' Shambhu continued,

73

The king, who is the lord of Kamarupa, is my supreme devotee. O devas! Go and tell him that this task will be accomplished soon. The great king, Sudakshina, is the lord and king of Kamarupa. In particular, he is my devotee. Let him continue to worship me. The wicked daitya, known as Bhima, has obtained a boon from Brahma. But there is no doubt that I will kill the one who has made you suffer.

After this, all the delighted gods left that place. They went and told the great king what Shambhu had said. After informing him, the devas were filled with great delight.

In order to protect and ensure his welfare, Shiva affectionately went near his own devotee, along with his ganas. But he remained hidden. Meanwhile, the lord of Kamarupa started to immerse himself in deep dhyana in front of the parthiva lingam. Someone went and told the rakshasa, 'The king has started some *abhichara* against you.'[30] Hearing this, the rakshasa became angry. He seized a sword and rushed towards the king, desiring to kill him. Seeing the parthiva lingam there, the rakshasa thought, 'He must be doing something with this. Therefore, I will use force to kill the king and destroy all his ancillary stuff.' Thinking this, the extremely angry rakshasa spoke to the king, 'O evil-souled king! What are you doing now? Please tell me the truth. Otherwise, it is certain that I will kill you.' Hearing these words, the lord of Kamarupa quickly thought about this in his mind, full of faith in Shiva.

---

[30] *Abhichara* means magical practices, typically with evil intent.

What is going to happen is certain to happen. No one can contest it. Everyone is subject to prarabdha karma and Shiva is said to be the one who determines prarabdha. The compassionate Shankara is certainly present in this parthiva lingam. He will act for my sake. Who is this rakshasa? Where has he come from? It is true that he always acts according to the pledge he has made. Bhagavan Shiva is truthful to his pledge.

Hence, resorting to fortitude, he continued to perform dhyana on Shankara, the divinity. Bound by the bonds of truth, the king thought this in his mind and addressed the rakshasa in slighting words, 'I am worshipping the divinity Shankara, who protects his own devotees. He is without aberrations and is the lord of everything, mobile and immobile.' Hearing the words of the lord of Kamarupa, Bhima's body trembled in rage, and he said,

I know about your Shankara. What will he do to me? Is your desire to win based on his strength? Until I have seen Shankara, your protector, you can think of him as your lord and serve him. O king! However, once I have seen him, everything will become clear in every possible way. Therefore, keep this image of Shiva far away. Otherwise, there is no doubt that you will face a reason for fear now. I am terrible in my valour, and I will lay my fierce hands on your lord.

Hearing these words, the lord and king of Kamarupa, whose faith in Shankara was firm, quickly addressed him, 'O vile one! O wicked one! I will never let go of Shankara. My lord is the best of all, and he will never leave me.' Hearing the words of the king, whose atman was in Shiva, Bhima laughed. The rakshasa quickly replied to the king, 'He is mad. He constantly begs. Does he know what he looks like? How can yogis be intent on protecting their devotees? Reflect on this in your mind and always maintain a distance. Your lord and I will fight.' The best of the kings was firm in his devotion to Shambhu. He replied fearlessly to Bhima, who constantly brought misery to the world.

Bhima laughed and hurled his terrible sword towards the parthiva lingam. 'Now behold your lord's strength, which brings happiness to devotees.' Saying this, the immensely strong rakshasa laughed aloud. As soon as the sword touched the parthiva lingam, Hara manifested himself from within the parthiva lingam. 'Behold. I am Bhimeshvara. For the sake of protection, I have manifested myself. I had previously pledged that I would always protect my devotees. Therefore, swiftly witness my strength, which brings happiness to devotees.' Saying this, he used Pinaka[31] to slice the sword into two fragments. At this point, the rakshasa hurled a trident. But Shambhu shattered the wicked one's trident into fragments. He next hurled a spear towards Shambhu. Shambhu used his arrows to instantly shatter this into a hundred thousand fragments. He hurled a jagged javelin towards Shambhu. But Shiva used his trident to immediately reduce it to bits as small as sesame seeds. Thereafter, there

---

[31] Shiva's trident. Sometimes, pinaka also means Shiva's bow.

was an extremely terrible battle between the rakshasas and Shiva's ganas, causing grief to those who witnessed it. At that moment, everyone on earth was agitated. The oceans and all the mountains trembled. The devas and all the rishis were anxious. They told each other, 'Our prayers to Shiva have been in vain.' Narada arrived before Shankara, the destroyer of misery. He lowered his head, joined his hands in salutation and prayed, 'Please pardon me, O Lord! Please forgive me. You are causing confusion. Why use an axe when a blade of grass will do? Please kill him quickly.' Thus entreated, the lord Shambhu used the humkara weapon to reduce the large number of rakshasas to ashes. Shankara burned down all the rakshasas in an instant. While all the devas watched, Shiva's rage swiftly burned down the army of rakshasas, just as the fire from a forest conflagration burns down a forest. No one could see Bhima's ashes. He was burned down, along with his companions. No one ever heard of his name again. As a result of Shiva's favours, peace was obtained. Indra and all the other devas and the entire world went back to their natural states. The blaze that arose from Mahesha's rage spread from forest to forest. The ashes of the rakshasas were scattered in all the forests. Many kinds of useful herbs originate from this. There is no task that cannot be performed with these ashes. The devas and sages especially requested Shambhu,

O Lord! For the happiness of the worlds, please remain established in this place. This is an awful region that has brought misery that cannot be fought against by people. If they see you, there will be welfare here. You will have the name Bhimashankara and will ensure every kind of success. This lingam must always be worshipped and will counter every kind of sin.

Shambhu, who brings welfare to the world, was requested in this way. The self-ruling one, affectionate towards his devotees, happily remained established there.

In the famous Jyotirlingam Shloka, Bhimashankara is said to be in the region of Dakini. Where is Dakini? It is said that the Bhimashankara jyotirlingam is near Pune. Perhaps it is, and the Bhimarathi river flows nearby. Though the present temple isn't that old, there are temples and cave carvings all around. There are forests, and this is obviously an ancient place of worship. The one near Pune is naturally famous. However, what does one make of the word dakini? It can mean the south (dakshina) and by not too great a stretch, Maharashtra can be construed as the south, at least in those days. But dakini could also mean a place where *dakinis* were worshipped.[32] In that case, one should look for a place with a tantra tradition. More importantly, how does one reconcile Kamarupa with Maharashtra unless one comes up with a very convoluted explanation? Kamarupa squarely places the lingam in what is Assam today. Indeed, there is a Bhimashankara jyotirlingam near Guwahati. Not too many people have heard of it, not even those who reside

---

[32] The word *dakini* has several meanings, including some that are specific to *tantra*. Here, we can simply take it to mean minor feminine deities.

in Guwahati. There are few visitors and no temples. At least there isn't a temple dedicated to Shiva. There is one for Ganesha and another for Vishnu. Bang in the middle of the forest, with the lingam amid a waterfall, it is worth a visit, regardless of which is the real Bhimashankara jyotirlingam.

Ramesha in Setubandha

Everyone knows the basic story of the Ramayana; Rameshvara is connected to that story.

Earlier, Vishnu, loved by the virtuous, assumed an avatara on earth. Ravana, extensive in his use of maya, abducted Sita. He took Janaka's daughter to his own residence in Lanka. Searching for her, Rama arrived in the city known as Kishkindha. Becoming Sugriva's friend, he killed Vali. He remained there for some time, searching for her. He held consultations with Sugriva, Lakshmana and others. The son of the king sent the monkeys in four directions. Hanuman was the foremost among the ones who were sent to search her out. The supreme monkey went to Lanka. From his words, Raghava got to know that Sita had been taken to Lanka. He also received Sita's crest jewel and was delighted. Along with the lord among monkeys, Lakshmana, the leader Sugriva, and a sacred force of strong vanaras who numbered eighteen *padmas*,[33] Rama went to the shores of the ocean. The salty ocean could be seen in the southern direction. Rama went

---

[33] A *padma* is a very large number, specifically 1000 billion.

Rameshwaram

there and stationed himself on the shore. Loved by Shiva, he was served by Lakshmana and the vanaras.

> Alas! Where has Janaki gone? When will I go and meet her? This army of vanaras must be made to cross the fathomless ocean. The rakshasa who held up the mountain is extremely strong and valiant. His fortress, known as Lanka, is impossible to penetrate. Indrajit is his son.

Remaining on the shore with Lakshmana, these were his thoughts. Angada and the other residents of the forest comforted him.

Meanwhile, Raghava, supreme among Shiva's devotees, wanted some water and lovingly spoke to his brother, Lakshmana. Rama said, 'O brother! O Lakshmana! O lord of heroes! I am thirsty and wish for some water. Please ask a vanara to quickly fetch me some.' Hearing this, vanaras dashed off in ten directions. They brought water. Prostrating themselves, they stood in front of him and spoke. The vanaras said, 'O Lord! Please accept the water. Obeying your command, we have brought it. It is tasty and the best. It is cool and revives life.' He was extremely pleased and cast a glance of compassion towards them. Hearing this, Ramachandra accepted the water. He was about to drink the water that had been brought. But because of Shiva's wish, he remembered something. 'I have not seen Shambhu yet. How can I drink water? He is Paresha, my lord, who bestows every kind of bliss.' Saying this, the supreme descendant of the Raghu lineage drank the water. After this, the descendant of the

Raghu lineage worshipped a parthiva lingam. He performed *avahana* and other rituals and devised sixteen kinds of *upachara*.[34] Following the norms, he lovingly worshipped the divinity, Shankara. He prostrated himself and made efforts to satisfy him with divine hymns. Full of joy and devotion, Rama prayed to Shankara. Rama said,

O Lord! O Shambhu! O Mahadeva! You are always affectionate towards your devotees. Please save me. I am your devotee, and I have sought refuge with you. My mind is distressed. O one who enables a person to cross over the ocean of samsara![35] This water is fathomless. The rakshasa known as Ravana, is immensely strong. He is extremely valiant. In fighting a battle, this army of vanaras is fickle. How will my task be accomplished? How will I get my beloved back? O one excellent in vows! Therefore, your task is to help me. O Lord! Without your help, my task is impossible to accomplish. Ravana is one of your own. Therefore, in every possible way, he is impossible to defeat. He is insolent because of the boons he received from you. He is immensely brave and has conquered the three worlds. I am also your servant, and I am subservient to you in every possible way. O Sadashiva! Thinking about this, you should be partial to me.

---

[34] *Avahana* is the act of invoking a deity; *visarjana* is the act of releasing the deity. *Upacharas* are offerings made during worship. The number of articles usually offered is sixteen.

[35] *Samsara* is the worldly cycle of death and rebirth.

Bhimashankar

OMKARESHWAR

Rameshwaram

SRISAILAM

TRIMBAKESHWAR

In this way, he prayed and repeatedly prostrated himself. He said, 'Victory to Shankara, the one who punishes the wicked. Victory.' Thus, using mantras and dhyana, he praised Shiva. He again worshipped him and bent down before him. His heart was flooded with love, and the voice choked in his throat.

The divinity Shankara was greatly pleased. Maheshvara appeared on the shores of the ocean, along with his companions. He was a mass of energy. He manifested himself in this sparkling and wonderful form. Maheshvara was satisfied with the devotion in Rama's heart. Shiva told Rama, 'All will be well. Ask for a boon.' Seeing that form, all of them were purified. Devoted to Shiva's dharma, Raghava worshipped him. Rejoicing, he praised him in many kinds of ways and prostrated himself. He prayed for his victory against Ravana. Maheshvara's mind was pleased with Rama's devotion. He spoke again, affectionately. 'O great king! May you be victorious.' He obtained the permission for victory bestowed by Shiva. With his head lowered and his hands joined in salutation, he prayed again. 'O Lord! To purify the world, please remain established here. O Shankara! If you are satisfied, please do this to help others.' Thus addressed, Shiva assumed the form of a lingam there. On earth, he became famous under the name Rameshvara. As a result of his powers, Rama crossed the ocean easily. He swiftly killed Ravana and the other rakshasas and got his beloved back. Rameshvara's greatness is wonderful and unmatched on earth. It bestows objects of pleasure and emancipation and always grants devotees what they wish for. If a person devoutly bathes Shiva in Rameshvara with the divine water from the Ganga, he becomes a *jivanmukta*.[36] He enjoys all the objects of pleasure in this world, which are difficult even for devas to obtain.

Nagesha in Darukavana

There was a rakshasi named Darukaa who was insolent because of a boon obtained from Parvati. Her husband, Daruka, was supremely strong. Along with many other rakshasas, he created carnage among the virtuous. He destroyed sacrifices and dharma in the world. Along the shores of the western ocean, there was a forest that was prosperous in every possible way. In every direction, it extended for sixteen yojanas. Whenever Darukaa went to the forest for her own pleasures, the ground there was covered with trees and every other kind of accompaniment. Devi gave Darukaa that forest to look after. They remained there and caused fear for all the others who were there. Because of Daruka rakshasa and his wife, Darukaa, all the people suffered. They went and sought refuge with the sage Ourva. The people said, 'O Maharshi! Please grant us refuge. Otherwise, the wicked ones will kill us. Other than you, there is no one else on earth who can offer us refuge. On seeing you, all the rakshasas run a long distance away. Shiva's blazing energy always radiates in you.' Ourva replied, 'The rakshasas may be supremely strong. But if they cause violence to other beings on earth, they will

---

[36] A person who is liberated while still alive.

Nageshwar

lose their own lives. When sacrifices are destroyed, all the rakshasas will lose their lives.' Devas learned about this curse. Therefore, they made efforts to fight against the enemies of the devas.

Seeing this, the rakshasas resorted to consultations. The rakshasas said, 'What should be done? Where will we go? We are fighting and are being killed. They are fighting and are not being killed.' Unable to think of a means, they were constantly miserable. Rakshasi Darukaa also got to know that a calamity had presented itself. Therefore, she spoke about the boon granted by Bhavani.[37] Darukaa said, 'When

---

[37] Devi Parvati.

I worshipped her earlier, Bhava's wife bestowed a boon on me. If you so wish, you can come to the forest with me. I obtained a boon from her. Let the rakshasas be taken to the forest that is in the water[38] and remain there happily.' Hearing the rakshasi's words, the rakshasas were filled with joy. They lost their fear and spoke to each other. 'She is blessed. Our queen has been successful in saving our lives.' There were people who had suffered many miseries on account of the rakshasas earlier. Meanwhile, they arrived there to fight alongside the devas.

The rakshasas took everything to the city, which was land in the middle of the water. The rakshasi praised Devi and uttered words of 'Victory'. Without any fear, all of them remained there in the middle of the ocean. They remained inside the city in the water and amused themselves. The rakshasas never came to earth. Scared of the sage's curse, they remained in the water. They seized people travelling in boats and took them to the city. They hurled some of them into prisons in the city and killed them. Because of the boon granted by Bhavani, the rakshasas were fearless. Remaining there, they again started to cause suffering wherever they could. Earlier, people constantly faced fear on land. Now, they constantly faced fear in the water. Sometimes, the rakshasi emerged from the city in the water. She obstructed the path. Standing there, she made people on land suffer. Meanwhile, many beautiful boats arrived there, and all of

---

[38] Clearly, there was an island. The boon was that they couldn't be harmed in the forest.

them were full of people. Seeing these boats, the rakshasas were delighted. Those crooked ones quickly rushed there and seized them. Those immensely strong ones brought them to the city. They hurled the people into prisons and bound them up in strong fetters.

Among them, there was a Vaishya named Supriya. He was auspicious in conduct and always devoted to Shiva. He was loved by Shiva. He never remained without worshipping Shiva. He followed Shiva's dharma in every possible way, wearing bhasma and rudraksha as ornaments. When he could not worship, he would not eat. There too, the Vaishya was engaged in worshipping Shiva. In that prison, he taught many people how to worship Shiva using a parthiva lingam. According to their own desires, all of them worshipped Shiva. They used many modes, depending on what they had seen and heard. While they were there, some of them sat in excellent asanas and immersed themselves in dhyana. Some of them delightedly worshipped Shiva in their minds. Their leader created a parthiva lingam, followed the norms and directly worshipped Shiva. There were others who did not know about the methods. They remembered the supreme mantra, *Namo Shivaya*, and immersed themselves in meditating on Shankara. In this way, as the Vaishya worshipped Shiva, six months passed without any impediments.

On one occasion, one of the evil-souled rakshasa's attendants saw Shankara's beautiful form in front of him. He went and informed the king of the rakshasas. The king of rakshasas, Daruka, quickly arrived there. Though he was strong, he was agitated and inquired about Shiva. Daruka

asked, 'O Vaishya! Who are you meditating on?' He replied,
'I do not know.' Hearing this, the rakshasa became angry
and sent rakshasas, asking them to kill him. Instructed by
him, they swiftly went there to kill him with many types of
weapons. Seeing them arrive, Supriya was scared, but his
mind was fixed on Shankara. He cheerfully remembered
Shiva and repeatedly chanted his name. When he prayed this
way, Shambhu emerged from a cavity. Amid this, Shiva's
form was a mass of radiance. He was with his attendants.
On seeing him, Supriya worshipped him, and Shambhu
was pleased to be worshipped in this way. He gave him a
weapon named Pashupata. He himself killed the bulls
among rakshasas and all their followers and he destroyed
their equipment. It was wonderful. Shankara protected his
devotee and killed the wicked. Having killed all of them, he
bestowed a boon on the forest. 'In this forest, the dharma
of the varnas, Brahmanas, Kshatriyas, Vaishyas and Shudras
will always be observed. The best among sages will be here,
never with *tamas* qualities. They will propound Shiva's
dharma and practise Shiva's dharma.' At this time, the
rakshasi Darukaa, who was distressed in her mind, praised
Devi Parvati. Pleased, the Devi asked, 'What will I do?' She
replied, 'Please save my lineage again.' Parvati said, 'I will
protect your lineage.' Saying this, she quarrelled with Shiva.
Shiva saw that Devi Parvati was angry. However, the lord
was bound by the boon he had conferred. Therefore, he
cheerfully said, 'Do what you wish to.' Parvati was extremely
happy to hear the words spoken by her husband, Shankara.
Parvati said,

Your words will come true when it is the end of the yuga. Until then, it is my view that creation should possess the qualities of tamas. You should prove that the words I speak will come true. This rakshasi Darukaa is, in fact, a devi, and she is my Shakti. She is the strongest among all the rakshasis. Let her rule over a kingdom of rakshasas. These wives of rakshasas will give birth to sons.

Shankara said,

O beloved! If you say so, please listen to my words. To protect devotees, I will happily remain in this forest. Whoever is seen to cheerfully establish the dharma of varnas here will become the emperor. Otherwise, when Kali Yuga is over and a new Satya Yuga starts, there will be a lord of men famous under the name of Virasena, Mahasena's son. He will be extremely valiant. He will be my devotee, and he will be able to see me. When he sees me, he will become an emperor.

In this way, the couple laughed and spoke to each other. They remained in that place and brought greatness to it. In the form of the jyotirlingam, Shiva came to be named Nageshvara. Devi became Nageshvari. Both are loved by virtuous people.

In the beautiful region of Nishadha, Virasena was born into a Kshatriya lineage.[39] He was the son of Mahasena and

---

[39] When Shiva spoke to Parvati, this was in the future tense. By the time the story was narrated in the Puranas, the incident belonged to the past tense.

was loved by Shiva. With a parthiva lingam, he worshipped Isha. Virasena performed extremely difficult austerities for twelve years. Shankara manifested himself and spoke.

Make a wooden boat that is in the shape of a fish and smear it with tin. I will create Yogamaya and give her to you. Accept her. With her and your men, enter the boat. Use that to go and enter the cavity I created. Enter the place and worship Nageshvara. You will obtain Pashupata there. Use that to slay the rakshasi and others.

Nageshwar

In this way, Shiva conferred a boon, and Virasena became capable of doing everything. In this way, the divinity originated as Nageshvara, the lord of all the jyotirlingams. In the form of the jyotirlingam, he satisfied all the desires in the three worlds.

Vishvesha in Varanasi

Among jyotirlingams, perhaps the most famous is the–Vishveshvara jyotirlingam. But first, a little bit on Kashi, also known as Avimukta. Everything that can be seen in the world is only a material object. His nature is one of consciousness and bliss. He is without transformation and eternal. He is *kaivalya*,[40] but he desired a second. In this way, the saguna form, known as Shiva, originated. He divided himself into two, differentiated as masculine and feminine. The masculine form is known as Shiva and the feminine form is spoken of as Shakti. Both Purusha and Prakriti were created from a form whose nature was consciousness and bliss. The form from which they originated could not be seen. Unable to see their mother and father, Prakriti and Purusha were filled with great doubt. A voice arose from the Nirguna Paramatman. 'For the sake of excellent creation, you must undertake austerities.' Prakriti and Purusha replied, 'O Lord! O Shiva! A place does not exist for austerities. Following your instruction, where will we base ourselves to undertake the austerities?' Just then, an auspicious energy spread, extending for five kroshas. This became a beautiful city, equipped with every possible object.

---

[40] The ultimate goal—absolute unity.

Kashi

It was created and sent by Nirguna Shiva, and it remained in the firmament, near Purusha.

Desiring to create, Vishnu established himself there. Resorting to dhyana, he tormented himself through austerities for a very long period. As a result of his efforts, many streams of water started to flow. They enveloped the void, and nothing could be seen. Vishnu saw this and thought, 'What is this wonderful thing that can be seen?' Seeing this wonder, he shook his head. Just then, an earring fell in front of the lord. From this, the great *tirtha* of Manikarnika[41] originated. That

---

[41] *Tirtha* is a pilgrimage site or holy place, and Manikarnika literally translates to 'the jewel from the ear'.

expanse of five kroshas was floating in the flood of water. At that time, Nirguna Shiva quickly held it up on his trident. Vishnu slept there, along with his wife, Prakriti. Following Shiva's command, Brahma originated from the lotus in his navel. As a result of Shiva's instructions, he started on a wonderful act of creation. He created the cosmic egg with its fourteen worlds.[42] Sages have said that the expanse of the cosmic egg extended for fifty crore yojanas. 'In this cosmic egg, bound by karma, how will beings obtain me?' With this thought, he released Panchakroshi.[43]

> It is my view that this brings auspiciousness to the world and destroys karma. It manifests emancipation. Kashi leads to the bestowal of jnana. It is extremely loved by me. The lingam of Avimukta has been established by the paramatman himself. O one who has been born as my portion, you should never abandon this kshetra.

Saying this, Hara himself released Kashika from his trident and brought it down to earth, in the world of mortals. When Brahma's day ends, it is certainly not destroyed. Shiva holds it up on his trident then. When Brahma starts his act of creation again, it is re-established. It is understood to be Kashi because it drags out karma.[44] The lingam of Avimukteshvara

---

[42] Seven upper regions and seven lower regions.

[43] The expanse consisting of five (pancha) kroshas.

[44] That is, it destroys karma. Based on *karshana*, drawing out or dragging.

is always established in Kashi. It bestows emancipation on people, even if they have committed great sins. *Sarupya* and other forms of emancipation can be obtained elsewhere.[45] But it is only here that living beings obtain *sayujya*, the best form of emancipation. Those who cannot find a destination can find it in the city of Varanasi. Panchakroshi is extremely sacred and destroys the sin of killing crores of people. All the immortals desire a death here. What needs to be said of others? It bestows objects of pleasure and emancipation. It is always loved by Shankara. Brahma always praises it, as do Vishnu, the siddhas, yogis, sages and all the others in the three worlds.

The lord of Kailasa has tamas on the outside and sattva inside. He is nirguna. But assuming gunas, he is famous under the name of Kalagni.[46] Prostrating himself several times, he spoke the following words. Rudra said,

O Vishveshvara! O Mahesha! There is no doubt that I belong to you. O Mahadeva! Please show me your compassion. I am your son, and that of Amba.[47] For the welfare of the world, please remain established here always.

---

[45] The terms mentioned refer to different levels of emancipation. *Salokya* is the ability to reside with the Lord, *samipya* is proximity to the Lord, *sarupya* is to be like the Lord in form and *sayujya* is identification with the Lord. For those unfamiliar with Shaiva dharma, Rudra is not the same as Shiva.

[46] The fire of destruction.

[47] The mother, Parvati.

O protector of the universe! O lord of the universe! I am praying to you to be a saviour.

Avimukta[48] controlled his atman and beseeched him repeatedly. With tears of joy flowing from his eyes, he spoke to Shankara:

O lord of devas! O Mahadeva! O excellent medication against the ailments of time! You are truly the lord of the three worlds. You are served by Brahma, Achyuta[49] and others. O divinity! Please accept the city of Kashi as your capital. For this unthinkable pleasure, I will remain here, immersed in dhyana. Other than you, there is no one else who can bestow emancipation, no one else who can grant wishes. Therefore, for the sake of welfare, always remain here with Uma. O Sadashiva! Save all beings from this ocean of samsara. O Hara! Please accomplish the task of the devotees. I am praying to you repeatedly.

Vishvanatha Shankara was entreated in this way. For the welfare of the world, the one who rules over anyone remained there. The day Hara arrived in Kashi is the time from which Kashi became the best place of all.

On one occasion, Devi Parvati was filled with great delight. Desiring the welfare of the world, she asked Shankara

---

[48] Rudra
[49] Vishnu

about the greatness of the two Avimuktas.[50] Parvati said,
'Out of compassion towards me and desiring the welfare of
the worlds, you should tell me about this kshetra's greatness.'
Hearing the devi's words, the lord of the universe and the
lord of the devas replied to Bhavani, to ensure pleasure for all
beings. Parameshvara said,

O fortunate one! You have asked a virtuous question. This
will bring happiness and auspiciousness to the world. I
will accurately describe to you the greatness of the two
Avimuktas. Varanasi is my most secret kshetra. To grant
emancipation to beings, I am always present here. In this
kshetra, siddhas have always resorted to my vratas. They
have many kinds of forms and always desire my world.
There are some who have resorted to the supreme and
great yoga of Pashupata, which the Shruti texts describe
as bestowing objects of pleasure and emancipation as
fruits. They have conquered their atmans and their
senses. O Maheshvari! Residing in Varanasi, giving up
everything else, always appeals to me. Listen to the clear
reason for that. There are two kinds of people who obtain
emancipation: my devotees and those who possess jnana.
They do not need tirthas, and what should be done and
what should not be done is the same for them. Wherever
they might die, they become jivanmuktas. They will
certainly obtain emancipation. These are my conclusive

---

[50] By the two Avimuktas is meant the city of Kashi and the
Vishveshvara lingam.

words. However, there is something special about this supreme and excellent tirtha, known as Avimukta. O Devi! O supreme Shakti! All the varnas and ashramas—children, young people and the aged—as long as they die in this city, there is no doubt that they are liberated. Pure or impure; a virgin or married; a widow or barren; whether there are menstrual defects or not, irrespective of whether she has delivered and irrespective of whether she has been through *samskaras*—if a woman dies in this kshetra, there is no doubt that she is liberated. Those born from sweat (worms and insects), those born from eggs, herbs and plants and those born from wombs—when they die, their prospect of emancipation here is like that in no other place. O Devi! One doesn't have to depend on jnana. One doesn't have to depend on devotion. One doesn't have to depend on karma. One doesn't have to depend on donations. One doesn't have to depend on samskaras.[51] One doesn't have to depend on dhyana either. One doesn't have to depend on chanting names. One doesn't have to depend on worship or good birth. My kshetra bestows emancipation on any human who resides here. When he dies here, it is certain that he will obtain emancipation. O beloved! Such is my divine city. It is the most mysterious among everything mysterious. O Parvati! Brahma and the others do not know about its greatness. That is the reason this great kshetra is

---

[51] Sacraments, or the different acts of purification one goes through during one's life.

known as Avimukta.[52] When it comes to bestowing emancipation, it is superior to Naimisha and everything else. The truth is the dharma of the Upanishads. Moksha is what Upanishads talk about. The learned know that the kshetra of Avimukta represents the essence of all tirthas and Upanishads. A being may enjoy many kinds of desire and engage in many activities for pleasure—as long as life is given up in Avimukta, it is said that there is liberation. It is better for a man to commit one thousand sins and become a *pishacha*[53] than to perform 1000 sacrifices and go to heaven without having been to the city of Kashi. Therefore, every effort must be made to visit the city of Kashika.[54] There, the sages meditate on Sadashiva in his unmanifest lingam. A man undertakes austerities for the sake of fruits. But it is I who bestow all those fruits on him. People who give up their bodies here do not suffer from the bonds of karma. Having obtained *sayujya* with the paramatman, they subsequently obtain the desired destination. Brahma, along with devas and rishis, Vishnu, Surya and the great-souled ones, worship me and no one else. A man may be addicted to material objects or may not be interested in dharma. However, if he dies in this kshetra, he does not have to enter samsara again. What can be said of those without a sense of ownership, patience, based on sattva and devoid of insolence, those

---

[52] A place that grants emancipation (*mukti*).

[53] *Pishacha* is a kind of demon that feeds on flesh.

[54] Kashi.

who do not begin anything without offering everything to me? After thousands of births, a person is born as a yogi. If he desires supreme emancipation, he should wish to die here. There are many lingams here, established by devotees. O Parvati! All of them yield objects of desire in this world and emancipation thereafter. It is said that in four directions, this kshetra extends for five kroshas. When a being dies here, it bestows immortality. If a person who has not committed a sin dies here, he obtains emancipation instantly. If a person who has committed a sin dies here, he must go through several bodies. He experiences those hardships and obtains emancipation subsequently. If a man commits a sin in the kshetra known as Avimukta, it is certain that he must go through pain for 10,000 years. It is only after he has enjoyed the consequences of the sin that he obtains emancipation. I have thus told you about those who are inclined towards wicked conduct. Knowing this, a man must properly serve Avimukta. Even in hundreds of crores of *kalpas*,[55] the fruits of karma are not exhausted. The fruits of karma performed, good or bad, must be enjoyed. Exclusively wicked deeds in this world lead to hell. Exclusively good deeds lead to heaven. A mix of the two is said to lead to birth as a human. O

[55] A *kalpa* is one of Brahma's days. There is destruction at the end of Brahma's day, when the *kalpa* ends. When night is over and Brahma wakes up again, creation starts afresh and there is a new *kalpa*.

Maheshvari! The sections on *karmakanda*[56] speak of three kinds of bonds of karma—*sanchita, kriyamana* and *prarabdha.*[57] Everything accumulated across previous births is said to be *sanchita.* What this body is about to enjoy is spoken of as prarabdha. There are good and bad deeds that are being performed in this birth, now. The learned know this as kriyamana. Prarabdha karma must be exhausted by enjoying the consequences. There is no other way. However, the other two kinds of karma can be destroyed through worship and other things. Other than in Kashi, all kinds of karma cannot be destroyed. All the other tirthas are easy to reach. However, the city of Kashi is extremely difficult to reach. If a person lovingly saw Kashi in a former life, then he can reach Kashi and die there in the present birth, not otherwise. If a man reaches Kashi and bathes in Ganga, sanchita and kriyamana karma are destroyed. It is certain that prarabdha karma cannot be destroyed without enjoyment. One dies and is reborn. That is how it is exhausted. If a person has visited Kashi in the past[58] and has committed a sin thereafter, the seed is so strong that he is taken to Kashika again. All the sins are then reduced to ashes. Therefore, to destroy their roots, a man must certainly go to Kashi. If residence is arranged for even a single Brahmana in Kashi, that is like

---

[56] *Karmakanda* usually means rites and rituals, as opposed to *jnanakanda*, the pursuit of *jnana*.

[57] Respectively, accumulated, ongoing and matured.

[58] This might mean a former life or the present life.

the benefactor himself dwelling in Kashi. Therefore, he obtains emancipation. If a person dies in Kashi, he does not have to undergo rebirth.

Kashi

As stated by Shiva himself, there can be no better explanation for the greatness of Vishvesha in Varanasi.

Tryambaka on the Banks of Goutami

In earlier times, there was a supreme rishi, famous under the name of Goutama. His wife was named Ahalya, and she was supremely devoted to dharma. In the southern direction, there is the mountain known as Brahmagiri.[59] For 10,000

---

[59] This has to be the one in Nashik district in Maharashtra.

years, he tormented himself through austerities there. On one occasion, there was a terrible drought that lasted for 100 years. It brought misery to people. Not a single moist sprout could be seen anywhere on the surface of the earth. No water, required for living beings to sustain life, could be seen. Sages, humans, animals, birds and deer fled in ten directions. On seeing this, the rishis spent that extremely terrible time immersed in pranayama and dhyana.

For the sake of Varuna,[60] Goutama himself engaged in auspicious austerities. For six months, he was immersed in pranayama. To bestow a boon, Varuna appeared before him and spoke the following words: 'I am pleased with you. I will grant you a boon.' Goutama prayed for rain. At this, Varuna replied to the sage. Varuna said, 'How can I oppose the command of devas? You know everything. Please ask for something I can do for you.' Hearing these words, Goutama, who wished to do a good turn to others, replied, 'O lord of the devas! If you are pleased, and if I am to be given a boon, then you should give me what I have asked for. Since you are the lord of waters, you should give me water. It should be eternal and divine, such that it always yields fruits.' Thus, as requested by Goutama, Varuna said, 'Dig a pit here.' He dug a pit that was the length of a hand. Varuna filled this with divine water. After this, Varuna, the lord of waters, spoke to the sage Goutama. Varuna said, 'O great sage! This water will be eternal, and this place will become a tirtha. It will be famous on earth under your name. Donations, oblations,

---

[60] The god of water, the oceans and the rivers.

austerities, sacrifices to gods and shraddhas for ancestors will all be inexhaustible, as long as they are performed here.' Saying this and being praised by the maharshi, the deva vanished. Having been successful in helping others, the sage Goutama was happy. The nature of excellent people is that they cannot tolerate the miseries of others. They counter it for others, even if they must go through hardship themselves. Trees, gold, sandalwood and sugarcane exist on earth only for the sake of others. The four sacred pillars that support the earth are a kindly person, a person not touched by insolence, a person who helps others and a person who has conquered his senses. Thus, Goutama obtained water, which was so very difficult to get. Following the norms, he performed *nitya* and *naimittika karma.*[61] For the sake of oblations, the lord among sages sowed vrihi (paddy), barley, nivara (wild rice) and many other things. There were many kinds of grain and many kinds of trees. There were many flowers and fruits there. Hearing this, thousands of other rishis arrived there. Many animals, birds and other living beings also arrived. Since the water was perennial, there was no hardship on account of the lack of rain. The rishis engaged in auspicious rites in the forest, and many of them resided there along with their disciples, wives and sons. In the course of time, they sowed grain. Because of Goutama's powers, that forest was filled with joy.

---

[61] *Nitya karma* consists of rites performed every day. *Naimittika karma* consists of rites performed on a special occasion and *kamya karma* consists of rites undertaken for desired fruits.

On one occasion, Goutama sent his own disciples to fetch water. They faithfully went there with their water pots. There were many wives of the rishis who had gone there for water. When the disciples went and reached the water, they saw them and restrained them. 'We are wives of rishis. We will take it first. Go far away. You can take the water later,' they reprimanded them in this way. They returned and reported this to the rishi's wife, Ahalya. The ascetic lady comforted them. She took them with her and went there. Taking the water herself, she gave it to Goutama. Using this water, the supreme rishi performed the rites every day. The angry wives of the rishis reprimanded her. Crooked in their minds, they returned to their own cottages. In front of their husbands, they reported the opposite of what had happened. Under the control of their own karma, hearing their words, the supreme rishis became angry with Goutama. Angry and wicked in intelligence, they worshipped Ganesha[62] with many kinds of offerings, desiring to create impediments for Goutama. Ganeshvara was pleased and appeared before them. Subservient to devotees and desiring to grant them fruits, he addressed them in these words. Ganesha said, 'I am pleased with you. Ask for a boon. What will I do?' Hearing his words, the rishis spoke to him. The rishis said, 'If a boon is to be given by you, let Goutama be expelled out of the hermitage. Please arrange it so that the rishis censure him.' When they asked for this, the one with the head of an elephant laughed. The destination of the virtuous spoke to

[62] Ganesha removes impediments as well as creates them.

them cheerfully, so as to make them understand. Ganesha said,

O rishis! All of you listen. It is not right to do this now. Anger when no offence has been committed leads to harm. It is not good to cause misery to those who have done a good turn in the past. If such misery is inflicted, it leads to destruction. One strives while undertaking austerities to obtain excellent fruits. Discarding those auspicious fruits, one should not, on one's own, strive for what is injurious.

The intelligence of those excellent sages was deluded. Therefore, hearing those words, the rishis said the following: 'This is what you must do, nothing else.' Thus addressed, the Deva Ganesha spoke the following words:

A wicked person never becomes virtuous. A virtuous person never becomes wicked. Earlier, because of the loss of food, you faced hardships. It was Maharshi Goutama who gave you this happiness. You now wish to inflict misery on him. In this world, this is not right and must be reflected on in every possible way. Deluded by the power of your wives, you are not acting in accordance with my words. There is no doubt that all this will lead to his welfare. The supreme rishi will again grant you happiness. Crossing him is not right. Please ask for another boon.

Hearing the words of the great-souled Ganesha, the rishis did not pay any heed to what he said. Under the control of his devotees,[63] Shiva's son spoke, indifferent towards those rishis who desired something wicked. Ganesha said, 'I will indeed do what you have asked for. What is going to happen will certainly happen thereafter.' Saying this, he vanished.

Goutama did not know about the wickedness of the sages. With a happy mind, along with his wife, he performed the nitya karma. Meanwhile, the wicked rishis had been given a boon. There was vrihi and barley in Goutama's field. Ganesha assumed the form of a feeble cow and went there. As a result of the boon, he went there, with his body trembling, and started to eat the vrihi and barley. As a result of destiny, Goutama arrived there at the time. The compassionate one tried to restrain the cow with a blade of grass. Touched by the blade of grass, the cow fell to the ground and died instantly, while the rishi looked on. The rishis and the inauspicious wives of the rishis were hiding themselves there. All of them shrieked, 'What has Goutama done?' Goutama was amazed and distressed in his mind. He summoned Ahalya and spoke to her miserably. Goutama said, 'O lady! What is this and how has it happened? Maheshvara must be angry. What is to be done? Where will one go? The sin of slaughter has presented itself.' Meanwhile, the Brahmanas reprimanded Goutama. The wives of the Brahmanas caused sorrow to Ahalya with their harsh words. The evil-minded disciples and sons also reprimanded Goutama, uttering words of 'Shame!' The rishis said,

---

[63] A deity must always listen to a devotee.

Your face cannot be seen. Go. Leave this place. If one sees the face of a person who has killed a cow, one must immediately bathe. As long as you are in the middle of the hermitage, the fire and the ancestors will not accept anything that we offer. Therefore, along with your family, go somewhere else. Do not delay. You have committed the sin of killing a cow.

Saying this, all of them threw stones at him. They caused him pain and addressed Ahalya in harsh words. Struck and reprimanded by those evil ones, Goutama spoke the following words: 'O sages! I will leave this place and go and reside somewhere else.' Saying this, Goutama left that spot. He took their permission and went and made his hermitage at a place that was one krosha away. 'You cannot perform any rite as long as this curse is on you. You do not have any rights to any rites from the Vedas, meant for devas and ancestors.' Goutama, the noble sage, was extremely miserable. After spending a month there, he requested the sages, 'You should have compassion towards me. Please tell me what I should do. Please tell me how my sin can go away.' Thus addressed, those Brahmanas did not say anything. All of them got together and, remaining in one place, spoke to each other. Goutama remained some distance away; his head humbly bowed down. Full of humility, he asked those excellent rishis, 'What will I do now?' The rishis replied,

Until you are freed from the sin, you will never be purified. Therefore, to purify your body, you must perform *prayashchitta*.[64] Circumambulate the earth thrice, proclaiming your sin aloud. After that, return here and observe a vrata for a month. It is also ordained that if you go around Brahmagiri 101 times, you will be purified. Or go to Ganga and bathe there. Create one crore parthiva lingams of the divinity and worship them. When you bathe in Ganga thereafter, you will be purified. You can also go around this mountain eleven times and bathe a parthiva lingam with water from 100 pots. That way, too, you will be purified.

When the rishis addressed him in these words, he agreed. 'I will go around the mountain and worship a parthiva lingam. O illustrious ones! Please grant me permission.' Saying this, the noble rishi circumambulated the mountain. The supreme sage then constructed a parthiva lingam and worshipped it. The virtuous Ahalya also did all this, while the disciples and the disciples of the disciples served them both.

Along with his wife, the rishi worshipped Shiva. Shiva was pleased and manifested himself, along with his ganas. Shiva, the ocean of compassion, was pleased and said, 'O great sage! I am pleased with your excellent devotion. Ask for a boon.' He saw the beautiful form of the great-souled Shambhu. Delighted, he prostrated himself before Shankara and praised him. He prostrated himself and uttered words of praise several times. He then joined his hands in salutation and stood there. Goutama said, 'O divinity! Please cleanse me of sin.' Hearing

---

[64] A rite of atonement.

the words of the great-souled Goutama, Shiva was pleased even more and addressed him in these words:

> O sage! You are blessed. You have accomplished your objective. You have always been cleansed of sin. All those evil-souled ones have deceived you. When people see you, they become cleansed of sin. Since you are constantly devoted to me, how can you be a sinner? O sage! Those evil-souled ones have harassed you. They are sinners and wicked in their conduct. They are like killers. On seeing them, others are also becoming sinners. Those who are ungrateful can never be saved.

Saying this, the lord Shankara, who bestows happiness on the virtuous and punishes the wicked, told him in detail about their wicked conduct. Hearing Shiva's words, the rishi's mind was amazed. He devoutly prostrated himself before Shiva and, joining his hands in salutation, spoke again, 'O Mahesha! Those rishis have done me an immense good turn. Had they not done that, how would I have been able to see you? Blessed are those rishis. They have done something even more auspicious for me. As a result of their wicked conduct, my great selfish objective has been achieved.'

Casting a compassionate glance towards him, Shiva said, 'O rishi! You are blessed. Since you know that I am pleased, ask for an excellent boon.' Goutama, best among sages and devoted to Shiva, joined his hands in salutation. He bowed his head and addressed Shankara, 'O Lord! What you have said is true. O lord of the devas! If you are pleased with me, please give me Ganga. Please do a good turn for the world. I prostrate myself before you.' Desiring the welfare of the world, Goutama prostrated himself before the lord of devas. Shambhu, affectionate towards his devotees, granted the sage the boon. The water of the Ganga assumed a supreme feminine form.

The best among rishis bent down and praised her, 'You are blessed. You have purified the world. O Ganga! Please purify me. Otherwise, I am certain to descend into hell.' Shambhu said, 'Listen. You always do what is beneficial to everyone. O Ganga! Follow my command and purify Goutama.' Hearing the words of Shambhu and Goutama, the purifying Ganga, full of devotion towards Shiva, spoke to Shiva. Ganga said, 'O Lord! After purifying the rishi and his family, I will return to my own abode.' Thus, addressed by Ganga, Mahesha, affectionate towards his devotees and intent on the welfare of the world, again addressed Ganga. Shiva said, 'O goddess! You will remain here until the advent of Kali Yuga.' Hearing the words of her lord, Shankara, Ganga, the supreme river who purifies, replied, 'O Lord! O Maheshvara! O destroyer of Tripura! If my greatness surpasses that of anyone else, I will remain here. O Lord! In your beautiful body and along with Amba and your ganas, you must also remain here, near me.' Hearing her words, Shankara, affectionate towards his devotees and intent on the welfare of the world, spoke to Ganga again, 'O Ganga! Listen. I am not separate from you. Nevertheless, I will remain here, and you must also stay here.' Hearing the words of Paramesha, her lord, Ganga was pleased in her mind and worshipped him.

Meanwhile, devas, ancient rishis, many tirthas and diverse kshetras arrived there.[65] All of them lovingly worshipped Goutam, Ganga and Girisha. All the immortals, Hari, Brahma and the others, joined their hands in salutation and happily praised them. Ganga and Girisha were pleased and spoke to them. 'O best among gods! We wish to bring you pleasure. Ask for a boon.' The devas said, 'O lord of the devas! O best among rivers! If you are pleased with us, as an act of compassion towards us and for the pleasure of humans, remain here.' Ganga replied, 'For everyone's pleasure, why don't you also stay here? After cleansing Goutama, I will return to wherever I came from. O gods! How can I be known to be distinct from you? If you can establish that, there is no doubt that I shall remain here.' All of them responded:

Guru is the best well-wisher for everyone. When Guru is in Simha *rashi*, there is no doubt that all of us will come.[66] O supreme river! After purifying and cleansing the world for eleven years, we will become polluted. Therefore, we will come to you to cleanse ourselves. O best among rivers! To show us a favour and for the pleasure of the world, please remain here with Shankara. As long as Guru is in Simha, we will also remain here. We will bathe in you thrice a day and see Shankara. When we do this, there

---

[65] Tirtha and kshetras are both sacred places of pilgrimage. But typically, a tirtha is a place where one descends into water.

[66] Guru (Brihaspati) is the planet Jupiter. That is, when Jupiter is in the constellation (*rashi*) Leo (Simha).

is no doubt that we will be cleansed of all our sins. With your permission, we will then return to our own regions.

Thus, requested by them and by Maharshi Goutama, Shankara lovingly remained there, and so did the best among rivers. Ganga is named Goutami[67] and the lingam is known as Tryambaka. Both became famous under these names and destroyed great sins. Since that day, whenever Brihaspati enters Simha, all the tirthas and kshetras, all devas, all rivers and lakes, Ganga and the other rivers, and Vasudeva and other devas remain on the banks of Goutami. As long as they remain there, they cannot yield fruit in their own regions. They regain those fruits when they return. The jyotirlingam is famous under the name of Tryambaka. It is instated along the banks of Goutami and destroys great sins. Full of devotion, if a person sees the jyotirlingam named Tryambaka, worships it, prostrates himself and praises it, he is freed from all sins.

When Ganga was requested by Goutama himself, she swiftly descended from Brahmagiri. The flow is issued from the branches of an udumbara tree (the fig tree). Goutama, the famous sage, bathed there and rejoiced. There were other maharshis who were Goutama's disciples. They too arrived there, and, having bathed, were filled with delight. That place became famous under the name of Gangadvara.[68] It

---

[67] Goutami Ganga is another name for Godavari. Tryambaka means the one with three eyes, Shiva.

[68] Gangadvara means door of the Ganga or gate of the Ganga. Gangadvara is usually identified as Haridvara. But this Gangadvara is clearly different..

is beautiful, and as soon as one sees it, all sins are destroyed. The rishis who challenged Goutama arrived there to bathe. However, as soon as she saw them, she instantly vanished. Goutama quickly went there. He praised Ganga repeatedly, joining his hands in salutation and lowering his head. He spoke to her. Goutama said, 'They were blind because of their insolence and prosperity. They may or not be virtuous. However, because of your sacred powers, you should show yourself to them.' Hearing the words spoken by the sage, the great-souled Goutama, Ganga's voice again arose from the circle that is the firmament.

O Rishi Goutama! You have spoken the truth, and these are auspicious words. Nevertheless, for the sake of protection, they must perform prayashchitta. Following your command and under your control, they must go around the mountain 101 times. It is only then that these evildoers will have a right, especially to see me.

Hearing her words, all of them did exactly what she had said. Dejected, they begged Goutama, 'You should pardon our crime.' When they did this, obeying her commands, Goutama created a place named Kushavarta, just below Gangadvara.[69] For his pleasure, she emerged from there again. Kushavarta became famous as an excellent tirtha. A

---

[69] Kushavarta tirtha or Kushavarta kunda is adjacent to Tryambakeshvara. This is the place where Godavari re-emerges, after disappearing into Brahmagiri.

man who bathes there becomes worthy of emancipation. He casts aside all his sins and obtains *vijnana*,[70] which is so very difficult to obtain.

This is how the Tryambakeshvara jyotirlingam originated.

Kedara in Himalaya

Nara and Narayana are spoken of as Hari's avataras.[71] In the region known as Bharata, they performed austerities in the hermitage of Badari. Shiva is subservient to his devotees. Requested by them, Shambhu arrived there every day in the form of a parthiva lingam, so that the worship might take place. In this way, Vishnu's two avataras worshipped Shambhu. The two devotees of Shiva, who were like his sons under dharma, did this for a long time.

On one occasion, Parameshvara was pleased and told them, 'I am pleased. Ask for a boon from me.' When he himself told them this, Nara and Narayana spoke words that would ensure the welfare of the world. Nara and Narayana said, 'O lord of the devas! If you are pleased and if a boon is to be given, please remain here in your own form, so that Shankara himself can be worshipped.' Hearing their words, Maheshvara Shankara remained there in the form of a

[70] *Vijnana* is knowledge and *jnana* is a synonym. When a distinction is drawn between *jnana* and *vijnana*, *jnana* is knowledge obtained from texts and through gurus. *Vijnana* is knowledge obtained through internal reflection and self-contemplation.

[71] Nara and Narayana are two ancient rishis. Badari is the Indian jujube, and this hermitage is known as Badarikashrama.

jyotirlingam, in Kedara in the Himalayas. He was worshipped
by them so that misery and fear might be dispelled for
everyone. He did this to do a good turn to the worlds and
to show himself to his devotees. Shambhu is himself present
there and is known as Kedareshvara. If one sees him or
worships him, he always bestows what is desired on devotees.
In ancient times, devas and rishis worshipped him there.
When Maheshvara was pleased, they obtained the fruits they
desired. The residents of Badari ashrama constantly worship
Bhava.[72] He always bestows what devotees wish for. From
that day, if anyone devotedly worships Kedareshvara, it is
impossible for him to be miserable, even in his dreams. When
he saw the Pandavas, he resorted to his maya. He assumed
the form of a buffalo and started to run away. When he was
caught by the Pandavas, he remained with his face facing
downwards. They caught hold of the tail and prayed to him
repeatedly. He is stationed there in that form and is known
under the name of Bhaktavatsala.[73] Part of the head went to
Nayapala and is stationed there in that form. He instructed
that he should be constantly worshipped in that incomplete
form. When he was worshipped, Shambhu himself bestowed
boons on them. Having worshipped him, the Pandavas left
happily. They obtained everything that their minds desired.

---

[72] Shiva.

[73] Literally, affectionate towards his devotees. Bhaktavatsala is
another name for Kedareshvara and explains why the lingam is in
the form of a hump. The incident with the buffalo occurred when
the Pandavas were on their final journey. The body of the buffalo
stretches from Kedarnath to Nepal, Nayapala.

They were freed from all misery. Hara is himself constantly present in that kshetra and is known as Kedara. The subjects of Bharata worship him. If anyone gives a *valaya* (a bracelet or a ring) there, he is loved by Hara. He approaches and attains Hara's form. If one sees that form, one is freed from all sins. If a person goes to the forest of Badari, he becomes a jivanmukta. If one sees the forms of Nara, Narayana and Kedareshvara Shambhu, there is no doubt that one obtains a share in emancipation. Those devotees who die on the road to Kedaresha are also emancipated. If one goes there, happily worships Kedaresha and drinks the water there, one does not have to undergo rebirth. In this land of Bharata, all beings who devotedly worship Nara, Narayana and Kedaresha are emancipated. He is the lord of everything, but he is especially the lord of this region. There is no doubt that Shambhu, known as Kedara, bestows everything desired.

Ghushmesha in Shivalaya

In the southern direction, there is the supreme mountain known as Devagiri (identified as Daulatabad). A Brahmana named Sudharma, born in the Bharadvaja lineage, lived close to it. His beloved, Sudeha, was devoted to following Shiva's dharma. Sudharma, best among Brahmanas, worshipped the devas and guests. He was always engaged in Shiva's rites. He was Shiva's devotee and loved those who were Shiva's devotees. He did not have a son and his wife's menstrual cycles were futile. However, since he possessed jnana about the nature of material objects, he did not grieve over this.

However, at not having had a son, Sudeha was miserable. Every day, she entreated her husband to make efforts so that they might have a son. He reprimanded his wife. 'What will a son do? Who is a mother? Who is a father? Who is a son? Who is a relative? Who is a beloved? There is no doubt that everyone in the three worlds is selfish. Use your intelligence to particularly understand this and do not sorrow.'

On one occasion, Sudeha went to a neighbour's house for a friendly conversation, but it resulted in a dispute. Because of her feminine nature, the lady of the house criticized her, saying, 'What are you proud of? You don't have a son. I have a son. My son will enjoy my wealth. Who will enjoy your wealth? There is no doubt that the king will seize your wealth. Shame on your wealth! Shame on you. Shame on your pride. You are barren.' Censured in this way, she returned home miserable and narrated everything to her husband. The Brahmana was extremely intelligent and did not grieve. He said, 'Let her say whatever she wants to say. What is destined to happen will occur.' Though she was repeatedly comforted in this way, she could not give up her grief. She entreated him anxiously. Sudeha said, 'You are loved by me, and you must do whatever you can to have a son. Otherwise, I will give up my body.' Sudharma remembered Shiva. The Brahmana flung two flowers into the fire that was in front of him. In his mind, he thought that the flower on the right would give him the desired son. Having taken this pledge, the Brahmana spoke to his wife. 'To obtain the fruit of getting a son, take one of the two flowers that are in front of you.' She thought in her mind, 'I will have a son. Let the flower my husband thought of come to me.' Saying this, she prostrated herself before Shiva. She then accepted one of the flowers. As a result of the delusion caused by Shiva's will, Sudeha did not pick up the flower her husband had thought of. Seeing this, the man sighed. He remembered Shiva's lotus feet and spoke to his beloved. Sudharma said, 'This has been ordained by Ishvara. It cannot but be otherwise. Cast aside your hopes. Serve the Lord.' Saying this, the Brahmana gave up his own hopes. He devoted himself to rites of dharma and performing dhyana on Shankara.

However, Sudeha did not give up her desire for a son. Full of love, she lowered her head, joined her hands in salutation and spoke to her husband. Sudeha said, 'If I cannot have a son, please listen to my words. Take another wife. There is no doubt that you will have a son through her.' Sudharma said, 'Do not create any impediments in the path of dharma now.' Though she was restrained in this way, she brought her younger sister home. Having brought her home, she requested that her husband marry her. Sudharma said, 'O beloved! You are telling me this now. But if she has a son, you will be jealous of her.' However, she clasped her hands and beseeched Sudharma again, 'I will not be jealous of my sister. Please follow my request. For the sake of a son, please marry her.' Accordingly, following the norms of marriage, the Brahmana married Ghushma. Having married her, the Brahmana requested her, 'O beloved! This is your younger sister, and you must always take care of her.' She served her sister as if she were a servant. Taking her sister's permission, the younger wife made 101 parthiva lingams every day. Ghushma worshipped them. Having done this, she flung them away into the nearby pond. In this manner, she worshipped Shiva every day. When 1100 images were complete, all the desired fruits were obtained. Through Shankara's favours, she had a son. Seeing him, the Brahmana was delighted. Devoted to the dharma of jnana, he was happy but not attached. However, Sudeha became fiercely jealous.

She could not tolerate Ghushma's happiness and started to oppose her. Since she gave birth to a son, everyone was constantly praising her. Sudeha was unable to tolerate the handsome child. Meanwhile, Brahmanas arrived, offering to bestow their daughters. Along with Ghushma, Sudharma followed the rituals and arranged for the marriage, filled with great bliss. All the relatives showed a great deal of respect for Ghushma. Seeing this, Sudeha's mind was inflamed with rage. When his son was married and brought the daughter-in-law home, Sudharma was enthused and displayed his joy to both his beloved wives. Ghushma was delighted, but Sudeha was full of misery. Ghushma said, 'These are your son and daughter-in-law, not mine.' Indeed, the daughter-in-law regarded her as the mother-in-law, and the son regarded her as his mother. The husband also loved the elder wife more, not the younger. Nevertheless, the elder had this impurity in her mind.

Sudeha thought, 'How can my misery be pacified? It is certain that the fire in my heart can only be pacified through Ghushma's tears of grief. There is nothing else that is causing my sorrow. Therefore, today, I will kill the son.' One day, the son and his wife were sleeping at night. Sudeha took out a knife and sliced off the limbs of Ghushma's son, took them to the pond and hurled them there. She flung them at the place where Ghushma flung the lingams every day. Happy, she returned and slept. In the morning, Ghushma woke up and performed her daily tasks. Meanwhile, Sudeha also happily went about the household tasks. In the morning, the daughter-in-law woke up and saw that the bed was wet with blood, with a few pieces of the body left. She went and asked her mother-in-law, 'Where has your son gone? The bed is wet with blood and a few pieces of the body can be seen. Woe is me. Who has done this wicked act?' She lamented about her beloved. Sudeha's mind was filled with joy, but externally, she displayed her grief. Ghushma heard her daughter-in-law's miserable words. However, she did not deviate from her vow and did not give up the daily worship of the parthiva lingam. There was not the slightest bit of mental anxiety in her. Her husband also continued to observe the vrata in the proper way. When the worship was completed at noon, she saw that terrible bed. Even then, there wasn't the least bit of grief in Ghushma. She did not grieve. Resorting to her fortitude, she immersed herself in Shiva.

With her mind in the same state as it used to be earlier, she took the parthiva lingam and chanting Shambhu's name, went to the bank of the pond. She flung the parthiva lingam in. As she was returning, she saw her son standing on the bank of the lake. The son said, 'I meet my mother. I was dead but have come back to life now. This is because of the power of your good deeds and Shankara's favours.' Seeing her son alive, Ghushma was not delighted, just as she had not been miserable earlier. At that time, Shiva himself appeared in front of her in the form of a mass of light. Satisfied, Mahesha spoke. Shiva said, 'I am pleased. Ask for a boon. The wicked one had killed him. I will kill her with the trident.' Ghushma bowed down and prostrated herself before Shiva, asking for a boon. 'O Lord! Sudeha is my sister. She must be protected by you. As soon as you are seen, no sins remain.' Hearing her words, Maheshvara was pleased even more. The ocean of compassion, affectionate towards his devotees, spoke again. Shiva said, 'O Ghushma! Ask for another boon. I will grant you what is beneficial for you.' Hearing this, she said, 'If a boon is to be given by you, for the protection of the worlds, please remain established here, under my name.' Maheshvara Shiva replied,

I will remain here, under your name. I will be known as Ghushmesha, the one who bestows happiness. My auspicious and extremely famous lingam, known as Ghushmesha, will originate here. This pond will always be a storehouse of lingams. This place will be famous in the three worlds under the name of Shivalaya. When it is seen, this pond will always bestow everything that is desired.

Saying this, Shiva assumed the form of the lingam named Ghushmesha. The pond became famous under the name of Shivalaya.

The Greatness of Shiva Ratri, and in Conclusion

In earlier times, there was a *bhilla*[74] in a forest. His name was Gurudruha. He was cruel. He went to the forest and hunted animals every day. On one occasion, the extremely auspicious Shiva Ratri arrived. However, the evil-souled one who resided in the forest did not know this. At that time, the bhilla's mother, father and wife suffered from hunger. He quickly seized his bow and left, desiring to cause violence to some animals. Such was his destiny that he could find nothing. The sun set, and he was filled with great sorrow. 'I have not obtained anything today. What will happen to my children and parents who are at home? I have a wife. What will happen to her? I must return only after I find something, not otherwise.' Thinking this, the *vyadha* approached a water body. There was a path that led down to the water. He went and stationed himself there. 'Some living being is certain to come here. Having killed it, I will happily return to my own house, successful in my objective.' With this thought, the bhilla climbed a bilva tree, taking some water with him.

When it was the first *yama*[75] of the night, a doe arrived. Seeing this, wishing to kill her, he quickly affixed a shining arrow to his bow. When he did this, some water and some bilva[76] leaves fell on a Shiva lingam that was underneath.

[74] Hunter, the same as *vyadha*.
[75] A period of three hours.
[76] Wood apple, sacred to Shiva.

This was the first yama, and he worshipped Shiva. On hearing the sound, the doe was scared. The doe asked, 'O hunter! What do you wish to do?'

The vyadha replied, 'My family is hungry. I will kill you now and satisfy them.' The doe said,

There is no doubt that I am blessed. You will be satisfied with my flesh, and my body will serve some purpose. Good merits are generated as a result of helping someone else. However, all my young children are at home now. I will entrust their care to my sister and husband and return. Know that my words are not false. There is no doubt that I will return to your presence again.

When she said this, the vyadha did not pay any heed to her words. Extremely surprised and scared, she again addressed him. The doe said, 'O hunter! I am telling you that I take this pledge. I will return to you from my own house.' When the doe took this pledge, the hunter believed her and said, 'Go home.' Happy, the doe drank the water and returned to the hermitage, where her home was. In this way, he spent the first yama without sleeping.

The doe had a sister. When this deer did not see her, she was worried. Following her trail, she arrived there, looking for water. On seeing her, the bhilla drew the string of his bow back, ready to shoot the arrow. As was the case earlier, water and leaves fell on Shiva's head. This was the second yama and there was a worship of Shambhu. Seeing him, the doe asked,

'What are you doing?' He repeated what he had said earlier. Hearing this, the doe also said what had been said earlier. The doe replied, 'O hunter! Hearing this, I am blessed. My having a body has been rendered successful. This body is temporary but can be used to do others a good turn. However, my infant children are at home. I will entrust them to the care of my husband and return here again.' The vyadha responded, 'I do not believe what you have said.' Hearing this, the doe took a pledge in Hara's name. Thus addressed, the hunter told the doe, 'Go.' The doe drank the water and returned to her own home. He also spent the second yama without any sleep.

Meanwhile, the third yama arrived. The stag was surprised at the delay. During that yama, intent on searching, he arrived and stood on the path that led to the water. The hunter saw a healthy deer and was delighted. He fixed an arrow to his bow and got ready to kill him. When he did this, because of his former radiant prarabdha karma, some bilva leaves were dislodged and fell on Shiva. It was his good fortune that this was the third yama of the night. Hearing the sound, the stag asked, 'What are you doing?' The hunter replied, 'For the sake of my family, I am going to kill you.' The stag said,

I am blessed that my well-nourished body will satisfy you. If the body is not used to do a good turn for someone, it is useless. If a person is capable but does not help another person, all his capability is futile. In the world hereafter, he goes to hell. However, I have infant children, and I must entrust them to their mother's care. I assure you that, having done this, I will return to you again.

The vyadha said, 'All those who came here were just like you. They took a pledge and left this place. But they did not return. They were deceivers. Having faced difficulty, you are also resorting to deceit. If I do this, how will I earn my living?' The stag replied, 'O hunter! There is no falsehood in me. Everything in the entire universe, including mobile and immobile objects, is based on truth. A deceiver's words dissolve his good merits in an instant. O bhilla! Nevertheless, listen to the truthful pledge that I am taking.' Hearing these words, the hunter said, 'Go and return quickly.' The stag drank the water and left.

Having made their pledges, all of them met at the hermitage. They spoke to each other and heard each other's accounts. Tied by the bond of truth, they made up their minds to return. They comforted the children and, without any hesitation, got ready to return. The elder doe addressed her husband. 'O deer! Without you, how will the children stay here? I am the one who took the pledge first. Therefore, I should go.' Hearing her words, the younger one replied, 'I am your servant. I must go now. You remain here.' Hearing this, the stag replied, 'I am the one who will go there. The two of you should stay here. Mothers protect their children.' Hearing the words of the husband, they did not think that this was in accordance with dharma. They cheerfully told their husband, 'Shame on life as a widow.' They entrusted the care of the children to others who resided there. All of them went to the place where the vyadha was. On seeing this, all the children also followed them. 'Our path must also be the one they have followed.' Seeing them, the hunter was delighted and fixed an arrow to his bow. Yet again, water and leaves fell on top of Shiva. Thus, the auspicious worship for the fourth yama took place. All his sins were reduced to ashes in an instant.

The two does and the stag spoke to the hunter, 'Please show us your compassion and make the bearing of our bodies successful.' Hearing their words, the vyadha was filled with wonder. As a result of the power of worshipping Shiva, he obtained jnana.

These deer are blessed. Though they are devoid of jnana, they should be revered. They are engaged in giving up their bodies for others. Having been born as a human, what have I achieved? I nourish my body by making the bodies of others suffer. Having committed sins since birth, where will I go? Shame on my life.

When this jnana was generated, he refrained from releasing the arrow. He said, 'O best among deer! Leave. Go in peace.' When he said this, Shankara was pleased. He showed him his own form. In his compassion, Shambhu touched the hunter and spoke to him. 'O bhilla! I am pleased with your vrata. Tell me about the boon you desire.' Having seen Shiva's form, the hunter obtained emancipation instantly. He fell at Shiva's feet and said, 'I have got everything.' Pleased with him, Shiva gave him the name of Guha. He glanced at him with eyes of compassion and gave him a divine boon. Shiva said,

You will now be able to enjoy the divine objects of pleasure you desire. You will reside in your divine capital, Shringaverapura. Without any impediments, your lineage will prosper, and you will be praised by even the gods. Rama will certainly come to your house. He is my devotee, and out of affection, he will become your friend. With your mind devoted to me, you will obtain emancipation, which is extremely difficult to get.

Meanwhile, having seen Shankara, all the deer prostrated themselves before him and were freed from their births as deer. On the mountain known as Arbuda, Shiva became Vyadheshvara Achaleshvara.[77] After having considered all the sacred texts and many aspects of dharma, the vrata of Shiva Ratri has been declared to be the best.

This book is about the twelve jyotirlingams. Each jyotirlingam is associated with a story, telling us how a parthiva lingam, worshipped by a devotee, became a jyotirlingam. Those stories have been recounted exactly as they are stated in the Puranas. Some stories are short, some longer. But since Shiva is everywhere, Shiva's lingams are everywhere too. As the Vyadheshvar Achaleshvara lingam illustrates, there are famous and sacred lingams not included in the list of the twelve jyotirlingams.

---

[77] *Achala* means someone who does not move. The Achaleshvara (Achalesha) temple is near Mount Abu, confirming the identification of Arbuda with Mount Abu. Achaleshvara and Vyadheshvara refer to the same lingam.

The Shiva Purana tells us that the total number of all Shiva's lingams cannot be enumerated. Everything on earth is full of lingams. Everything in the universe is full of lingams. All the tirthas are full of lingams. Everything is established on lingams. Everything that is seen, can be seen, described or remembered is Shiva's form. Nothing exists without him. Shambhu is worshipped everywhere by devas, asuras, and humans, in patala, heaven and on earth. To show his favour to the worlds, in the form of lingams, Shambhu pervades everything in the three worlds, along with devas, asuras and humans. For the welfare of the world, Maheshvara assumes lingams in various tirthas and other places. Wherever Shambhu's devotees remember him with devotion, he assumes an avatara there. Having performed the task, he remains established there. To do a good turn for the world, he devises his own lingams. If one worships those lingams, one attains siddhi. No number can be attached to the number of lingams on earth.

Most people are aware of these jyotirlingams. But they may not be aware of the *upalingams* (subsidiary or minor lingams) around these jyotirlingams.

The upalingam of Someshvara is said to be Antakesha. That upalingam is at the confluence of the Mahi with the ocean.[78] The upalingam of Mallikarjuna is said to be Rudreshvara. It is in Bhrigukaksha and brings happiness.[79]

---

[78] This probably pins it down to the Mahi Sagar district.

[79] Since Bhrigukaccha is clearly Bharuch, this causes a geographical problem. There are several Shiva temples (lingams) in Bharuch, but Mallikarjuna is far away.

The upalingams of Mahakala are famous as Dugdhesha. It is famous in the region around the Narmada and is said to destroy all sins. The upalingam of Omkara is famous as Kardamesha. It is near Lake Bindusara, and as fruits, it yields everything desired. The upalingam of Kedareshvara is Bhutesha, on the banks of the Yamuna. If a person sees or worships it, that is said to destroy great sins. The upalingam of Bhimashankara is said to be Bhimeshvara. It is famous and is in the region of Mount Sahya. It enhances great strength. The upalingam of Nagheshvara is said to be Bhuteshvara. It is on the banks of Mallika–Sarasvati. Beholding it destroys sins. The upalingam of Rameshvara is said to be Gupteshvara. The upalingam of Ghushmesha is said to be Vyaghreshvara.

Kashi

Kashi is on the banks of the Ganga and is famous because it bestows emancipation. It is known to be full of lingams. It is said to be the place where Shiva resides. The major lingam there is said to be Avimuktaka.[80] Krittivasheshvara is simultaneously in the form of an aged man and a young boy.[81] Tilabhandeshvara is in Dashashvamedha.[82] Sangamesha is said to be at the confluence of the Ganga and the ocean.[83] The one known as Bhuteshvara always bestows everything on devotees. The one known as Narishvara is near the Koushiki River.[84] Batukeshvara is on the banks of Gandaki. On the banks of the Phalgu River, Pureshvara is famous and bestows happiness. When men see Siddhanatheshvara, they obtain siddhi. The one known as Dureshvara is to the north of Pattana. The ones known as Shringeshvara and Vaidyanatha are also famous. The one known as Japyeshvara is at the place where Dadhichi fought. Gopeshvara, Rangeshvara, Vameshvara, Nagesha, Kamesha, Vimaleshvara, Vyaseshvara, Sukesha, Bhandeshvara, Humkaresha, Surochana, Bhuteshvara and Sangamesha are also said to be famous as the destroyers of great sins.

---

[80] The Avimukteshvara lingam is inside the Kashi Vishvanatha temple.

[81] This is near the Kashi Vishvanatha temple.

[82] The present Tilabhandheshvara temple is in Bangali Tola.

[83] The ocean should not be interpreted literally. It probably means the Varuna River, which is where the Sangameshvara temple is now, at the confluence of the rivers Ganga and Varuna.

[84] It is possible that this is a reference to the Arddha–Narishvara temple in Guptakashi.

Kumareshvara is on the banks of Taptaka (the river Tapi or Tapati.) Siddheshvara and Senesha are mentioned as being famous. Rameshvara, Kumbhesha, Nandishvara, Punjesha and Purnaka, in the region around the river Purna, are all famous. In ancient times, Brahmeshvara was established by Brahma in Prayaga at the tirtha known as Dashashvamedha. As fruits, they bestow the four objectives of human existence (dharma, artha, kama and moksha). In that way, Someshvara, which is also there, wards off all adversities. Bharadvajeshvara enhances the energy of the brahman. Shulatankeshvara directly grants whatever is desired. Madhavesha is also there and protects devotees. The famous Nagesha is in the city of Saketa (Ayodhya). It especially bestows happiness on those born in Surya Vamsha. Bhuvanesha is extremely famous and is in the city of Purushottama (Puri). The great lingam of Lokesha bestows happiness on everyone. Kameshvara is Shambhu's lingam, and Gangesha brings great purity. Shakreshvara and Shukrasiddha are there to bring welfare to the world. Vateshvara is famous and, as fruits, it yields everything wished for. Kapalesha is on the shores of the ocean, and Vakresha destroys all sins. Dhoutapapeshvara is directly in Parameshvara's portion. Bhimeshvara and Suryeshvara have also been mentioned. Nandeshvara is known to bestow jnana and is worshipped by the world. Nakeshvara is extremely sacred, and Rameshvara is also said to be like that. Vimaleshvara is also named Kantakeshvara. Dhartukesha is at the confluence of the river Purna and the ocean. As a fruit, Chandreshvara is known to bestow a radiance like that of the moon. Siddheshvara is said to grant every kind of wish. Bilveshvara is famous. So is Andhakesha, the place where, in ancient times, Shankara killed the daitya Andhaka. Shambhu assumed his own portion and is famous as Saraneshvara, always bestowing happiness on the worlds. Kardamesha is spoken of as supreme. Kotisha is situated on Mount Arbuda (Mount Abu). Achalesha is famous and always bestows happiness on people (this is also on Mount Abu).

Nageshwar

Nageshvara is always stationed on the banks of the Koushiki River. The one known as Ananteshvara is a store of welfare and auspiciousness. Yogeshvara and Vaidyanatheshvara are famous. Kotishvara and Sapteshvara are also spoken of as famous. Since the one named Bhadra is Hara himself, Bhadreshvara is famous. Chandishvara and Sangameshvara are also spoken about. Mattagajendraka lingam is in Chitrakuta, Brahmapuri.[85] Earlier, it was established by Brahma and granted prosperity and everything one desired. To the east of this is the lingam of Kotisha, which grants every kind of boon. The lingam named Pashupati is to the west of Godavari. To bring welfare to the worlds and happiness to Anasuya, the divinity manifested himself in the southern direction as Atrishvara.

Most people have heard of the twelve jyotirlingams but not the ones mentioned above. Today, an attempt to pinpoint them geographically is often futile. Shiva is everywhere, and his temples and lingams are everywhere.

---

[85] There is a Brahmapuri in Maharashtra, but that's not in Chitrakuta.

Mahadeva's Guide

Vibhav Kapoor

Om Namah Shivaya—ॐ नमः शिवाय—is the mantra that is on the minds, hearts and lips of every devotee waiting in line for a darshana of the Shiva lingam. Large groups of men, women and children chant in devotional grace as they wait to see a manifestation of the divine. Shiva, 'that which is not', is the ultimate reality (brahmān), the source, and what precedes and succeeds it—the nothingness from which everything emerges in this fabric of space and time. My journey through these jyotirlingams was a process of exploring the representation and experience of the living tradition of Shiva. Across all these sacred sites, people thrived on the relentless motivation of faith, belief and a longing to 'see' the manifestation of Shiva through the form of the lingam. Darshana, a Sanskrit word that means 'to see' or 'to view', is the central act when one visits a temple. The deity exists in a form accessed through the eyes, with the image central to the experience. Through darshana, there is a sense of connection with Shiva—a feeling of unity and harmony. As an artist and photographer whose life revolves around perceiving the world through vision, it felt like a divine blessing to have a darshana of these ancient lingams in these temples. It initiated me into a feeling of total surrender and vulnerability in the cradle of Shiva.

There was an individuality to this experience, as I was a photographer who was taking the photographs with a certain detachment from that of the observer, but it was also a collective experience with the people who were seeking the same goal of a darshana. Waiting in long queues, the pushing and pulling of fellow devotees, the constant heat and sweat—everything was an experience of a collective nature. The enormous crowds that I saw at these temples showed me the sense of community that is made possible by this religious and spiritual tradition. There was a sense of collective consciousness—meeting all the people on this journey and realizing that we are all very different in how our lives manifest and unfold in the material world but nonetheless similar in our spiritual instincts. It made me think of cosmic causality—the chain of causes and effects that got us all together at specific points and times. This cosmic causality is what governs our lives—society has given it different terms like fate, destiny, kismet, etc., and it is invisible. This is also a way I felt I experienced Shiva, Mahakala, as the manifestation of divine time. It was all part of divine timing to be in these places. After visiting the Kashi Vishwanath temple, we reached the Hyderabad airport to see the Mallikarjuna temple in Srisailam, which was about 240 kilometres from there.

We had no place to stay in Srisailam—we couldn't book anything online as it was a very remote town, and our travel agent had no local contacts. Standing at the baggage belt, my friend and I were confounded about what to do next and had no solid plan. While I was collecting my bag, an old lady approached us and started speaking to us about our purpose in Hyderabad. I told her that I was there to visit the jyotirlingam in Srisailam. She told me that her husband and she were locals from Hyderabad, and had come from Kashi, where they had also gone for a darshana. After getting comfortable in our conversation, I shared with her that I did not have a place to stay in Srisailam and had no prospects in mind. She and her husband started making phone calls to their friends in the region to help me. Eventually, she gave me her number, and we parted ways, hoping she would find me a place. A few hours later, I got a contact from her who ran a guest house in Srisailam, and they especially opened it up for my visit. It was divine cosmic timing for me to have crossed paths with Mrs Varalakshmi or pure coincidence, but a chain of cosmic causes and effects got us to that spot at that baggage belt at the airport in Hyderabad. It was experiences like these that shaped my whole journey— whether it was Mrs Varalakshmi at the Hyderabad airport, or Hamid bhai, our driver (one of the best drivers I have ever met who also drove Hilary Clinton when she visited India) in Maharashtra, who managed to get us through the traffic in the ongoing monsoon that lasted a week, or the father and

Srisailam

two sons who took us on a boat around the Om-shaped island in Omkareshwara, or Satya and Biku, the young boys whom I met at the Manikarnika ghat in Kashi who had grown up at the burning ghat. Each of these people and many more whom I fail to mention had a big role in how our journey progressed from one place to another. Being receptive to acts of kindness and the divine timing of confluences was how we managed to get through all these places and temples with ease and grace.

Thinking about such grace, the aesthetic experience of the temples was significant in shaping my spiritual experience. Through the virtue of their design and architecture, these temples present an aura. Many older structures are made using large blocks of stone, employing an interlocking technique that doesn't require cement to fix the system. They are also intricately carved with mythological scenery and narratives that depict animals, humans and the gods. Looking at the grandeur of these temples prompted me to think of them as a grand religious theatre, where worship and ritual are a performance done for the divine.

Baidyanath

Whether it was shouting 'Har Har Mahadeva' while running to the sanctum sanctorum in Baidyanath for a *shringār* darshana or being a part of the evening *aarti* at the Harsiddhi Mata temple in Ujjain, where pandits climb on sixty-foot-high lamps to light diyas, participating in the collective rituals felt like a performative art form. The sound and music also play a huge role in the aesthetic that shapes the spiritual experience.

One of the experiences that I distinctly remember was at the jyotirlingam in Grishneshwar. I reached the temple town in the evening, kept my bags at the hotel and walked straight to the temple. I was one of the last few people to enter the sanctum before the evening aarti began. At the aarti, the sound of the *nagara* (drum) pierced the skin of my physical eardrums, touching a spiritual plane. Bare-chested, with my eyes closed, my whole body started feeling lighter. I felt like I was moving in an upward, ascending direction against all the material forces of gravity, like evaporating water. For a moment, I had lost tension—I was not an 'I' but a selfless entity that became a vessel of an elevating consciousness. Because of the large number of devotees visiting these temples from all parts of India to seek such a feeling of oneness, these temples felt like geographic centres of an energy field—all the civilizational life in and around these sacred sites radiates from these temples. The ancient Ellora caves are located near the Grishneshwar jyotirlingam. Cut out of rocky mountains, these caves represent the Hindu, Buddhist and Jain traditions that have flourished in the region.

Grishneshwar

The beauty with which these caves were carved is extraordinary. There are thirty-four caves in all, a majority of which are dedicated to Hinduism, especially to Shiva. These caves exhibit sculptures of the different forms of Shiva and other mythological stories that concern the deity—Shiva's creative form as Nataraja, the marriage of Shiva and Parvati, Shiva in Padmasana and many more. One of the most common themes of representation in all the caves was a particular story of Ravana—Ravananugraha, meaning 'kindness to Ravana'. The folklore describes how Ravana, who became the biggest devotee of Shiva after this incident, was flying over the Himalayas when he spotted the beautiful Mount Kailash.

Omkareshwara

It was forbidden to fly over the mountain, and here he met Nandi, whom he disrespected along with mocking Shiva. He spread out all his arms and attempted to uproot the mountain from the ground. While this was happening, Shiva put his toe down on the mountain, trapping Ravana underneath it. Ravana cried out so loudly in tremendous pain that it shook the universe. On the advice of sages, it was here that Ravana started singing hymns in praise of Shiva for 1000 years. Pleased by his *tapasya,*[1] Shiva released Ravana's arms, forgave him and gave him the name of Ravana, which

---

[1] *Tapasya* means austerities, but has the nuance of scorching and purification.

Ellora

Ellora

means a 'terrifying cry'. The caves repeatedly depicted this story for both reasons—the devotion of Ravana as well as the supremacy of Shiva's power. Looking at and learning about this particular narrative offered me an eye-opening perspective on strength, humility and devotion.

Along with the glorious beauty of these temples and ancient monuments, the places where they are situated are also divinely beautiful. These temples are nestled in and around forests or on the banks of sacred rivers, like the Kashi Vishwanath temple on the Ganga and Omkareshwara on the banks of the river Narmada. The proximity of the temples and temple towns to these elements of nature made me ponder the natural world as a sacred entity. I felt a coherence with nature when visiting these places. I realized the cohabitation virtue between man and the natural world.

The remoteness of these locations also situates them in a primal setting—life exists in a very raw format. I still remember that day in Bhimashankara, when I went for a darshana. The Bhimashankara jyotirlingam is located on a mountain in the Bhimashankara Wildlife Sanctuary, which is part of Maharashtra's Sahyadari range. Since I made this trip in the auspicious Hindu month of Shravana, the monsoon season, it was continuously raining there. Maharashtra's monsoon is known for its robust downpour, which makes travelling slower and more complex, but also something that energizes the landscape. The flora is lush, and the water is constantly flowing—whether it's overflowing on the roads or generating small waterfalls that can be seen falling from the nooks and crannies of the mountains. There were two ways to get to the main temple—one was to take the public bus to the temple complex, and the other was to walk five kilometres up the hill to the shrine. Due to the vast crowds during Shravana, the bus was the slower and more crowded option. I thus decided to walk up to the shrine. It was one of the most fantastic walks I have ever taken: small ponds, lush green valleys and giant trees with branches like a dancer's arms covered the whole landscape. It was raining so heavily that I couldn't even see beyond ten metres, and since I couldn't see beyond a certain point, everything I saw seemed amplified. The thick layer of mist created a heavy blanket that veiled my vision, but it was also magically *presenting* the landscape as I walked through it. While doing this trek, I felt like I was fighting against the elements of nature in a primal sense of the word. I had to get through this channel of water to see Shiva. The mist and water all made sense in relation to the local story that I learnt about this jyotirlingam. It is believed that Shiva fought an evil demon at this place, and his sweat fell to the ground, thus creating the lingam. I couldn't help but imagine all that water and mist to be Shiva's sweat—a form of Shiva's blessing. Walking up that path was like reliving that mythological story—feeling the fight and flight of Shiva. When I reached the shrine, I saw that the darshana was happening for the lingam covered with a silver metallic crown—no one was allowed to see the lingam then. From walking through the rain and mist and thinking about Shiva's wrath to seeing the covered lingam, my whole experience at Bhimashankara was mystical. It felt like a place protected by the elements, which added to its otherworldliness. In the same Sahyadari hills of Maharashtra near Trimbak, where the Trimbakeshwar jyotirlingam is situated, I trekked on a mountain called Anjaneri.

Trimbakeshwar

This place is believed to be the birthplace of Lord Hanuman. According to mythology, Hanuman is believed to be the son of the wind (*vaayuputra*) and considered an incarnation of Shiva. The trek was a long, arduous climb up to the top of the mountain, where there was a temple dedicated to Hanuman. One of this trek's most interesting and exciting experiences was the gust of wind I felt while walking on this path. In the middle of the hike, there was a plateau point for about a kilometre before the steep climb to the top of the mountain began. At this point, I still remember feeling a kind of wind I had never experienced before. Like all the mist and water in Bhimashankara, it was the wind here in Anajaneri that took my breath away. The belief of the vaayuputra started ringing true—I became certain that the offspring of the element of air was born here. The divine timing of walking through these spaces, whether through the mist in Bhimashankara or the intense wind in Anjaneri, made even more apparent an incognizable play of chance—the presence of Shiva.

The mystical feeling of otherworldliness through the elements of nature was a recurring theme for my journey. In the southern state of Tamil Nadu, the town of Rameshwaram (where the Ramanathaswamy jyotirlingam manifests) is situated on the Bay of Bengal.

Along with this temple being located next to a great sea, water, as a cleansing and purifying element, plays a huge role in the darshana here. Before going to the main sanctum, I took a dip three times in the Bay of Bengal, which is about 100 metres away from the temple; this is called the Agni Tirtha. After this first bath, I went to the temple complex,

Rameshwaram

where I was washed by the water of the twenty-two wells called tirthas. These wells are meant to represent the twenty-two arrows that were in Lord Rama's quire. Only after cleansing oneself in these waters is one believed to get a proper darshana. Similarly, the jyotirlingam is also in the coastal town of Somnath in the state of Gujarat, which lies on the western coast of India.

This temple is situated on the Arabian Sea, so one can see and hear the waves while standing in the temple complex. In the present time, the authorities have created a wall that guards the temple against the pounding waves of the Arabian Sea, but standing there, I could imagine the waves having been much closer to the

Somnath

main sanctum at some point in history. Even then, the sound of the waves penetrated the walls of the temple complex and created a feeling of harmony between my mind, the energy of the lingam and the vast expanse that existed beyond the horizon. As mentioned earlier, the jyotirlingams are all located close to a water source, such as a river or sea. The element of water plays a fundamental role in the worship of Shiva, especially while doing a darshana of the lingam. *Jalabhisheka* is the act of pouring water over the lingam— water is offered to Shiva as it is believed to act as an energizing element and please the deity. I felt a connection between the element of water and Shiva, which was present in one form or another—rain, mist, river or sea—at all the places that I visited on this journey.

Thinking about such an elemental essence, Kashi (present-day Varanasi) is a place that represents a unique characteristic of Shiva. Kashi is a Sanskrit word that means 'shining' in English. Believed to be the abode of Shiva, it is also known as the city of death. This is a place where people choose to settle in the last stages of their lives and wait to die. The Hindus believe in the process of reincarnation—the soul takes on different bodies in each lifetime—and call this samsara, the cycle of death and rebirth. To attain absolute reality—Shiva—one has to go beyond and escape this cycle. It is believed that if one dies in Kashi, then one would not reincarnate, be released from samsara and go beyond the cyclical nature of time to attain moksha and reach Shiva. The Manikarnika ghat is the cremation ghat where it is believed that Shiva burnt his wife Sati's body and sat down to meditate. At that ghat in Kashi, I certainly felt an acceptance and embrace of death. The finality of life, the only objective truth that we all know, is apparent there in a way that shackles all the social, ethical and aesthetic connotations with which

I have been conditioned. The feeling of being there is one of total submission, a *tyaga*, a sacrifice of all material life and a desire to embrace Shiva through death.

While travelling across such a diverse set of places in India, I came across the different symbolic representations of Shiva. All the myriad experiences—collective consciousness, time, elements of nature and death—have expanded my artistic and social philosophy. As an artist, I have always attempted to equate the divine with the poetic. Through Mahadeva's guidance, I immersed myself in this sacred tradition of India and brought about poetry through the images I made, a sense of connection to all the places I saw. A trip like this happens once in a lifetime, but if I get a chance again to experience the energy of Shiva, I will do it all over again in all my lifetimes devoted to Shiva.

HERE AND EVERYWHERE

CONOR MARTIN

Before making this trip to take photographs of the jyotirlinga I went to the Pindari Glacier to meet a mentor who runs an outdoor leadership school in Ranikhet. He referred to India as 'a hunger driven society'. I express this because the more I travelled, staying with people and experiencing Indian life in various regions, the more accurately this characterization began to colour my perspective of the whole place where over a billion people are simply trying to survive day to day and generations are born, live and die on the street.

Coming from America, the sheer volume of people is a major cultural difference. In the West, privacy is valued as part of the social ethic. American life is typified by solitude, individualism and open space. In India this notion of personal space is a privileged concept that few people have the luxury to afford. This is evident in the photographs and for me this immersion with the Indian People is a large part of that transcendent spiritual experience. You have to lose your concept of self as you know it. It is a rite to get to Shiva.

As an Irish Catholic from the United States, I find that the cultural and religious traditions of India offer an alternative outlook. I have read the Bhagavad Gita and other Hindu concepts have reached me by way of Taoism, Existentialism and American Transcendentalism, but I wanted to experience what the people and the culture are really like. That is about tasting the atmosphere, walking the place, and meeting the people there.

I am skeptical that religious institutions are corrupt, hypocritical engines that run on conformity and fear to and extort the masses and am particularly disturbed by how comfortable most religions are with capitalism, which is particularly focused on the material rather than liberation from it. But it's the institutions which uphold the traditions, embodied by the art and performance rituals carried out in specific places like these temples. Because of this, there is a lot to learn in visiting such places.

Most significantly to me, the Hindu worldview seems more centered on the whole than the individual, and the sense of past, present and future is based on a notion of circular time rather than linear time. Much like the idea of the Trinity, Christianity's divine mystery, Shiva comes to us as the divine paradox. The God of creation and destruction, form and formlessness, the union of masculine and feminine, all and one. Something that, in my mind, is not unlike Tao, a friend with whom there are no hellos and no goodbyes, no thank you's and no apologies.

Shravana

We made our trip in July, which is Shravana, the holy month for Shiva. We are with the crowd, experiencing the maximum number of religious travellers one is likely to see at any time of the year. Large groups of pilgrims dressed in orange in chanting 'Lord Rhama' or 'Om Noma Shivai' resembled sports fans, coming to pay devotion day and night with a fervour that intensified inside the temple complex with exciting potency.

Half of the jyotirlingam authorities make you lock up your phones before entering and don't allowed photography inside the temples at all. In the other six, it is a matter of personal discretion. Permission for photography significantly impacts one's experience in a temple. Restrictions on taking pictures hurt our mission as documentarians but allows one to distinguish how people were conducting themselves based on different sets of rules affect the atmosphere and conduct in each place. Restricting photography makes these places much more peaceful without mobs facetiming or taking selfies. In the West, it is rare that phones aren't permitted in a cathedral but the custom when entering a 'sacred space' deters photography and phone usage. India is not that way and has such a visual culture that if people have their phones, particularly in a temple, they will be taking pictures. It is not seen as irreverent but as an affirmation. Sometimes, Pundits get upset, but that generally has more to do with money.

In Baidyanath Temple, the first place we travelled to, the masses of people praying, photographing and celebrating in the complex beneath large LED screens beaming out a live feed of the sanctum made me feel like I was participating in some cosmic sporting event, all part of one large organism: Team Shiva. Everybody was running through temples, getting slapped and prodded by men in fatigues, yelling, chanting, and trying to catch a glimpse of a silver Lingam. Water on the ground everywhere. This chaotic thing with the infinite seemed a strange force, like people were enslaved to the idea they had to come see this thing and put themselves through it. This was an overwhelming fate compelling people to be here and surrender themselves entirely to God.

Is this chaos a reflection of societal conditions? Is there an image of God across all faiths? Is that death? Is God a product of human derangement or can it exist outside of us? Amidst this chaos I wondered if your own conception of God can drive you mad? Entering into the sanctum in the evening was like stepping into a swift torrent. When we went down to the special VIP darshana, Pundits were throwing money on the Shiva lingam like a roulette wheel in an ancient back room in Monte Carlo. Making it rain within the sanctum sanctorum.

In this mass movement, there was no hallowed whisper. Everything going on embodied a chaotic relationship with the material. It occurred to me that these idols carved out of stone and adorned with flowers, some of them with clear countenance of a living thing, might be driving people mad. It was a raucous and violent scene, far from the stoic reserve of a Catholic church. There is an awesome power to these deities, along with the structures and these rituals that circulate around them. Eyed with fear and skepticism by many Christians, my encounters with these idols have filled me with a strange sense of incomplete oneness that comes out of reverence for the mystery. I can feel and respect this power and sense what it is about, and though my presence in this place was totally mystifying to the people around me, they always were appreciative of my curiosity and kindly welcomed me into the group.

Kashi Is the Capital of the World

Like Jerusalem, Kashi is a bustling ancient city all gearing to a spiritual plane powered by transcendence. There are temples everywhere and some of them are thousands of years old. There are salesmen and money changers everywhere, but the alleys, the architecture and wall paintings express the deeply personal character of the kind of faith people have in tradition and art. Even in the dusty blue streets of morning, you can feel everyone has some relationship with the eternal reverb.

Referred to as the City of Death, Hindus go there to die and be cremated so their souls escape the cycle of reincarnation. The climate and the sense of life and time are unique and unlike any place I have ever been. They say that it's older than history. There is a cremation ground below the jyotirlingam where families gather to perform their death rituals on the bank of the Ganges. I meet a young man who had spent his life on that ghat. He cooks his food with the fire they use to burn the bodies. He says that Shiva provides everything he needs there. He calls himself Real in English and says his name is Satya, meaning Truth. I look into his soul. He looks into mine.

'Everything is clean here,' he says, 'Pure. It is good for you to come here. You watch because you want to learn. This is cremation education.' We consume bhaang as men turn over burning bodies. He points to a stone step on the Ganges a few feet from where we are sitting beneath a tarp lean to. 'This is where Shiva sat and meditated when Sati, his first wife, burned herself. This is the eternal fire that has never gone out.'

He encourages me to take pictures and takes me to other temples and to the top overlooking the cremation grounds. I watch them carry the wrapped dead bodies and prepare them for cremation. Bodies burn amid piles of ash as generations of men stand by silently and others go about collecting orange tinsel cloth. Real talks to me about Aghori rituals and we discuss this relationship between the material and the ascetic path to moksha. It all makes me feel light and open. Purified. With the fire we stand in a portal between worlds; the unknown, life and death, time and the eternal. Here the presence of death is liberated from the drama of life. It is part of the cycle that cleanses the material world. There is a raging peace that comes with this detached awareness. It stirs something in your soul.

Real says, 'Cremation education. You must burn to learn. Be full of love. Know what I know. Born with nothing. We need nothing. We share everything. Real Baba, he does nothing. Just meditation. He doesn't fuck with sex. He doesn't fuck with money.'

Into the Forest

Far from Kashi, in the remote central southeast, the Mallikarjuna jyotirlingam sits on a hill along the Krishna

River. The village grew over time to support the temple's subsistence. Loudspeakers pipe out 'Om Namah Shivai' from sunup to sundown through the whole valley. The only economy is tourism generated by the temple and nearly all the local people worked to try and sell things to visitors. This is the case in most of these places.

Part of the custom for temple visitors is to descend the man-made steps to bathe in the Krishna. The sense of family and community there was very strong, seemingly heightened by the lack of infrastructure. One feels a deep sense of intimacy with the place due to its isolation. There was nothing else there but the force of this temple drawing people in like a supernatural magnet.

Because of tight control around the temple entry the place was crowded day and night with families visiting in large groups. They are there for darshana, which literally means to see the divine as embodied in the object or idol. This is a holy experience in Hinduism and as far as I understand you make an offering and see the idol and that is the sacrament. Often, these places are so crowded that people are waiting in packed lines for half the day just to catch its glimpse. Some places you can pay money to skip the free line and get to a shorter line, or pay a little more money to skip the line completely. Some places had no payment option at all. It all depends on the local pundits who make the rules and thus define the local culture.

In Srisailam, we paid and went to a waiting room with about a hundred people and they let us in in waves. There was an aarti going on at sunset and loud drums playing as we walked through the temple gate, which was completely gilded in silver. I felt a profound force rush through me, a unique feeling you experience when you are in an ancient place and catch a wave that gives you a completely different sense of time. Call this God. You could feel the presence of dark forces there in the quiet peace of the woods.

Rameshwaram is an island on the south-east tip of India. The day we got there we went out to Danushkodi which they say is where Ram built a land bridge connecting India to Sri Lanka. This is where the Arabian Sea and Bay of Bengal meet. The water is beautiful blue and clear. There is little more than a small village on the road up to the point, where people live in tarp dwellings after most of the structures were destroyed in a tsunami about twenty years before our visit.

Despite its beauty, the harsh conditions made the place feel barren and kind of hopeless. The beaches around town were inaccessible and choked with garbage. We walked around to check out the boats and get a sense of the space in the middle of the afternoon. I liked the place though I felt a strange sense of isolation rather than the feeling of soulful expansion I usually get when I am at the sea.

Pilgrims to Ramanathaswamy temple take a dip in the ocean at the town beach then go to the temple complex where they proceed to bathe in twenty-two wells before changing and doing darshana. I wasn't allowed to do darshana but I did bathe in the wells which was a very fun and beautiful ritual. We briskly moved through the maze of courtyards where pundits waiting for us at each well dipped buckets and doused us with sweet water as we proceeded along. Moving swiftly in groups it was a humorous and light-hearted experience.

As a non-Hindu in the south I wasn't allowed to go into the sanctum and look at the idol. So when Vibhav Kapoor (who has written the essay 'Mahadeva's Guide' in this book) went to the temple to do darshana I sat alone in an alcove and laid out my clothes to dry. The ornate and decorative porticoes as well as the large dramatic structure are characteristic of the southern temple. I sat there for a long time enjoying the beautiful sunny afternoon and meditated on things. This moment of exclusion permitted spiritual reflection. An irony that I, with a different conception of the almighty and meditation, had to savour.

In the late afternoon we drove out of town to the Devi temple which was on a hill looking across a flat plain leading to the ocean beyond. We got there right before it closed as the vendors were packing up. The light was perfect and the atmosphere was serene. We drank tender coconut water and planned to leave the next morning.

On the Road Through the Green

The main leg of our trip was a twelve-day drive from Mumbai through Maharashtra up to Ujjain in Madhya Pradesh. The first stop was Bhimashankara, the most remote of the jyotirlingams. There wasn't a town or village around, just fields engulfed in mist and rain. Everything was bursting thick green. The morning we got up to go to the temple, Kapoor and I saw a man walking in the field with a staff wearing just a dhoti with a rice sack on his head. He was a farmer or shepherd but in silhouette in the quiet mist he looked like a strange apparition. He was a farmer or shepherd but in the quiet mist, he looked like a strange apparition.

The place was ominously sequestered by the elements. Perhaps it felt that way because of the drama of the mist in the absence of cellular service. Despite the hordes of people being bussed to this strange black tower in the green forest and the sweat of Shiva covering us all, the experience of walking in patties through the rain was strangely reflective, like we had crossed an invisible barrier to get there. We left that day and drove to Trimbak, Kishore Kumar playing on the radio as we came down the mountain heading inland.

Trimbak is a small town close to Nashik that attracts a lot of visitors. There is a sacred bathing spot there which is the source of the Godavari River and the complex is well-preserved, public and clean. It is a living and active monument. The town has a medieval feel and is designed around the temple, which is surrounded by mesas that only a month before were arid desert but were now lush green and running over with waterfalls.

Between Nashik and Trimbak is a place called Anjaneri; a mountain believed to be the birthplace of the God Hanuman. Up there in the rain, wind ripping across the land and water cascading down the stone steps, the temple sits on the edge of the elements, 'the Wind and the Place', Hanuman's elemental Father and Mother. We were the last people up there during an afternoon storm and we reached the temple after most had gone down for the day. It was a spartan place and our experience getting up there embodied what one would attribute to the warrior God of self-discipline, strength and power.

Peace to Nashik, our last familiar stop where we stayed with family friends. As we continued deeper into the unknown inland the character changed dramatically from place to place. Ellora is a short drive east and is home to a UNESCO World Heritage Site as well as the Grishneshwar jyotirlingam. The village was the smallest and least developed of all the places we went to, and it was very poor. There are almost no modern structures except a few restaurants beyond a stagnant canal that runs behind the temple complex. People there were living out of their shops which were simply tarps rigged up along the dirt road leading to the temple.

The Real Thing

When we arrived in the evening, the man working at our hotel told us the aarti would begin in ten minutes, so we quickly dropped our stuff and went over. There were no phones allowed and there were only a few visitors, including a group of pious women who stayed together, separated from the men. The men had to take off their shirts to enter the sanctum, which was a small and intimate complex. The pundit was sitting cross-legged, singing, while the young priests played drums and worked with the fire. We went in, touched the Shiva linga and made our way out as they continued the ritual, watching with the people outside. The women were standing together in rows, looking at the idol, singing 'Om Namah Shivai' in a swift and high-pitched cadence. The temple security guard was violently pushing people, yelling and demanding they move to clear the way. The women stayed together, singing. The guard yelled as he pushed a man and slapped the flowers and coconuts out of a woman's hands. The drums continued. The women kept singing. A lone travelling priest blew his conch. The rhythmic pulse continued as the sunlight disappeared, then it all abruptly ended. With only a few dozen souls around, this place had an aura I hadn't experienced anywhere else, largely due to the intimacy and musical quality of the evening. After coming out and circling the temple seven times, the pandit said, 'Shiva lives everywhere, but he comes here to sleep.'

It was hard to ignore the thought that Ellora was being kept pure by starvation and economic deprivation. I felt it was the most difficult place for an outsider to photograph because there was no separation between the people and their way of life, which was the harshest small life I was confronted with the entire trip. Because of that the temple experience and the feel of everything were the most raw and intimate, free of the spectacle, throngs of people and more developed infrastructure which make a place impersonal.

The next morning we went to the Ellora cave complex, which consists of thirty-four individual temples carved into the face of a cliff dating as far back as the seventh century. Even though they were abandoned for hundreds of years the sculptures have their own pulse. They are alive. How do these empty dark holes dug out over a thousand years ago vibrate so intensely, as if waiting for a future reckoning? The locals are proud of their affiliation with these places. They want to talk with visitors and share their identities and histories with them. As we continued out of Maharashtra to Madhya Pradesh we began to slip into a much more remote area.

The Omkareshwara jyotirlingam is situated in a very rugged forest on an island in the Narmada River. All day music and prayer piped out of loudspeakers throughout the river valley where a series of bridges and walkways connect people in a circular pattern at two points from the island to the mainland. Wooden pontoon river boats rigged with ingenious handmade propellers welded directly on to generators serve as the local ferry system.

There is something savage and menacing about this place on the river. Because of the remote isolation contrasted with the scale of the temple and volume of visitors descending on the place there was a wild, liberated, vibrant feeling to it. No regulation. No pay to play access. No instruction. On the second night, after finally figuring out how to approach the temple, we were the very last people in line for darshana and the gates closed behind us. Being the last people in, our experience turned into an unrushed, solemn and intimate affair.

Carved into the wall was an image of Shiva crying in meditation which embodied the overwhelming feeling of wild suffering that I felt in this place. This was something very dark and powerful, not dark like the isolation of Bhimashankara, but a wild and crazed power. At sunrise, accompanied by the locals, we walked the circuit to the ruins on Mandhata's rocky crown which still function as a temple. Shortly after we left, they announced the construction of a corridor here. It may be good for the people and the economy, but the place will never be the same.

Ancient and Modern

Ujjain isn't more than a couple hours drive from Omkareshwara but it's a different world. The Mahakaleshwar jyotirlingam is sequestered by a modern corridor and sculpture garden recently built to accommodate tourists. It has a newborn shiny Las Vegas vibe with water fountains and large sculptures of a blonde-haired, blue-eyed Shiva. It was easy

Mahakaleshwar

to pay for darshana, and the entrance was lined with shoe stalls. The spectacle in Ujjain exuded a relaxed atmosphere, completely removed from the bustle of city life. Photographs were allowed from a distance, and the guards did not hurry us. The inside felt like an auditorium or sports arena. The corridor allowed easy access to the temple, but I didn't feel like I had experienced the city of Ujjain, and I felt a strange sense of displacement.

I was excited to visit Gujarat because I was intrigued by the history of the Muslim invasions, Zoroastrianism and the climate and proximity to the sea. Gujarat is quite rural, and it felt toned down compared to central India. Every place had an intimate feel to it, but was very poor and the natural spaces were harsh and usually filthy. The poverty was hard to see and engage with, and at this point, I was tired. By the time we arrived in Somnath and Dwarka, Shiva had pushed me to the limit of my heart. I was feeling strange and remote, tormented by the material world. I felt a long, long way from the transcendent spell I was under in Kashi.

Somnath, by the sea, was recently reconstructed after Independence. Passing through security gave me a deep sense of separation between this place and the world outside it. This compound ascends to a serene and higher plain, and the oceanside setting transcends time. The intricately carved deities on this liberated white stone seawall encase a sanctum of gold, south facing to the world's edge. Darshana was metered with a calm pulse of a drum. In the temple you can look out to the sea and taste the salt in the air. It was the first jyotirlingam to appear though it has been built up and torn down time and again. The temple itself is living history that embodies a whole worldview, a conception of the universe and an identity of a people that can never be destroyed. A glorious thought.

There wasn't much to the town itself, but people were open. A charismatic man stopped us in the streets and spoke to us for nearly an hour. He was pleased to meet an American and bought some soda and we drank it with him and his kids. His adoring wife looked at him with such reverent admiration. He said, 'You can always get more money, but meeting people and having experiences like this, you'll never get it again.' As a cow walked past us, he tapped the divine beast on the skull right between the eyes and said, 'All the gods are in the cow. But Shiva lives here.'

The surf on the Arabian Sea was intense, and the water looked like mercury as we headed west. The Dwarkadhish Krishna temple is divine. Going in for darshana and seeing all the sweets, leaves and greenery laid out in a banquet before a black-faced stone deity with eyes closed and adorned in bright silk in a hall of mirrors moved me to my core. My mind goes numb thinking about how to describe the grand beauty of the ornate carvings that covered every inch of that temple. Seeing the installation of food being offered and assembled by these people made me think of the hunger-driven society and the humility of religious sacrifice. It is a powerful thing to see people with so little offer so much.

The home of Krishna is welcoming and beautiful. The intense embrace and dark dramatic surrender I felt from the Shiva jyotirlingams on the mainland were not present in Gujarat. The Nageshvara jyotirlingam is a more recent construction to house the original lingam. The inside was airy and unadorned, more like a meeting hall with a relaxed atmosphere. Photography was permitted inside the temple, and vendors were selling goods next to the darshan line. In the field outside, large tents were set up for the arrival of an important pandit and it felt like we were at a fairground where a travelling show might have already happened or would be commencing later in the day.

There we took a boat to the island Bet Dwarka, the birthplace of Krishna. There has been a bridge under construction for years but the island is still only accessible by ferry boats. Several dozen people packed on to each vessel as all the women in the boat sang together crossing the channel. The island is a subsistence place with no cars and except for tourism around the temple most of it is a wildlife preserve. We did not hire a guide; we just walked around and got a sense of the place. It was peaceful. That will probably change once the bridge is finished. Then the ferry boats will probably slow down. It was a nice scene. A final scene.

The tourist apparatus makes things more comfortable. It provides a different narrative, creates a separation between the people living there and the visitors and alters the spectacle of the religious experience. This separation can take the edge off endemic poverty, but it doesn't solve it, and it creates something more homogenized and less personal. Religion is a manmade construct and wherever it exists, there will be exploitation and corruption. That is only part of the story however: the ironic twist. The devotion and beauty of what we saw, the rituals and places with immense power and the force that compels people is very real, alive, and has been sustained for millennia. This is not a basic and meaningless piece of trivia. It is an awesome and powerful fact.

My own spiritual belief is that God is everywhere and there is no separation within and without us. The designation of one place being more or less sacred than another is hard for me to accept though I cannot deny that in some places, the pulse beats much more intensely than others. Kashi is one of them. In fact, all of these Jyotirlingams are exceptionally powerful places. I would like to believe that this experience taught me that if you pay attention to this profundity, it can teach you to see deeper into all things, liberating your mind and spirit.

Because sometimes, the magic is there and sometimes, it is all smoke and mirrors and your expectations or lack of them will catch you off guard, but if you know Shiva you learn total surrender.

Scan QR code to access the
Penguin Random House India website